MARYLAND GHOSTS

Paranormal Encounters in the Free State

AMELIA COTTER

Second Edition:
First printing

First edition published by Black Oak Media, Inc. in 2012

Front cover photo and art:
Point Lookout Lighthouse, Copyright © 2010, 2015 by Mike Ricksecker

Back cover photo:
Jericho Covered Bridge, Copyright © 2012 by Jarid Kranz

Poem "her empty chair..." Copyright © 2012 by Amelia Cotter

1. Paranormal. 2. Ghosts—Maryland. 3. Haunted houses—Maryland.
4. Regional/travel—Maryland. 5. Maryland—History and folklore.

PUBLISHED BY HAUNTED ROAD MEDIA, LLC
www.hauntedroadmedia.com

United States of America

Praise for *Maryland Ghosts: Paranormal Encounters in the Free State*:

"Get ready for a haunted road trip through Maryland! The walls of those old buildings as well as the battlefields and other great landmarks *can* talk...and Amelia Cotter is listening. *Maryland Ghosts: Paranormal Encounters in the Free State* offers the history, the paranormal details, and the first-hand accounts that make us care deeply about these ghostly treasures. A great read throughout!"

–Jeff Belanger, author of *The World's Most Haunted Places*, Founder of Ghostvillage.com, and host of *30 Odd Minutes*

"Amelia does a fantastic job of telling the stories in such a way that you do not want to put the book down. Pour a glass of wine, crack the book open, and have a very enjoyable evening."

"Cotter does an excellent job of combining folklore, history, and personal accounts...It's a fun quick read that provides the opportunity to learn more. This book is great for anyone who lives in or plans to visit Maryland who would like to learn about the history in a fun and relatable way."

"This work makes a compelling read. Cotter includes images, dialogue, and real-time descriptions of investigations. The resources section at the book's end, full of websites with links that work, is a treasure for other ghost hunters who want more. The coffin factory chapter is especially spine-tingling, well-drawn, and disturbing!"

"THIS is the anthology of Maryland ghost stories that I've been looking for! All of the stories told are of personal experiences...this means you aren't getting the same old stories, rewritten and reworked from other print sources. I will keep my eye out for more books by her."

–Amazon reviews

Other titles by Amelia Cotter:

This House: The True Story of a Girl and a Ghost

Breakfast with Bigfoot (ages 3-6)

For Jen Kranz, Tif Smith, and all of my amazing friends in, from, and around Bel Air, Maryland—

Our wild adventures started it all!

her empty chair…

still telling

old ghost stories

ACKNOWLEDGMENTS

I would like to extend a special thank you to Mike Ricksecker of Haunted Road Media, Michael Kleen of Black Oak Media, Jeff Belanger, and my editor, Michelle Jacksier. A big thank you and hug are owed to my friends Jen and Jarid Kranz, for all of the work you've done to make this book possible! *Maryland Ghosts* is truly the product of a collaborative effort, so I would also like to extend my deepest appreciation to *all* of its contributors, for your incredible stories and pictures, invaluable input, and patience. Thanks to: Aunt Patty, Dad, Dani, Dina, Greg, Gwen, Kim, Kierstin, Melissa, Mom, Sarah, Susan, Terri, Tina, Uncle Bernie, Brenda Wilder Antlitz of G-Force Paranormal, Jenn Shape of Cecil & Beyond Paranormal, Margaret Perry Ehrlich and Ronda Dixon of Inspired Ghost Tracking, Samantha Kelley of K.R.I.P., and those of you who've chosen to remain anonymous. Much love goes to the rest of my friends and family, especially to my partner in life and crime, Jonathan, and my readers and fans for supporting me throughout this project. Last but certainly not least, I would like to honor the memories of my cousin, Eric Joneckis, and my favorite high school history teacher, Michael J. McAvoy, who were tireless supporters of my work and true inspirations in my life. May you both rock on in the great beyond.

TABLE OF CONTENTS

Beyond Ghosts: Other Encounters of the Paranormal Variety

Glimpses of the Supernatural: Brief Accounts and Memorable Moments

Resources and References

INTRODUCTION

Long before I was writing or doing any kind of serious ghost hunting, I was a nerdy kid growing up in the Maryland suburb of Bel Air in Harford County, avoiding getting into *real* teenage trouble by snooping around in the abandoned and allegedly haunted locales around the county and beyond. My late night expeditions with friends took me all over Maryland, and I began to see my home state in a whole new way.

Then, during and after college, I had the "privilege" of working at various haunted locations in Frederick and Washington Counties, where I would eat up the opportunity to ask around about ghost stories and learn about the history of each unique place.

While I consider myself a healthy skeptic, at least in most situations, I can't deny that after all the years of putting myself in places where paranormal encounters were possible, I have had quite a few incredible experiences.

Two of my favorite things in the world are sharing my stories with other people and listening to them share theirs. I also love Maryland—every one of its five regions, 24 counties, its history, people, and diverse landscapes. I have very warm and fuzzy feelings not only about Maryland being my home state, but also about the numerous stories and experiences I have shared here with others.

Maryland Ghosts has been, above all, a personal endeavor to gather and record the best of these stories that I've heard over the years from friends, family, fellow ghost hunters, and former coworkers around the state, as well as to research new stories and leads, making new friends along the way. I told perhaps my most powerful story in my first book, *This House: The True Story of a Girl and a Ghost*, and now in this one I will share a few more of mine as well.

As I was writing this book, I tried to channel a simpler time in the world of ghost hunting, a time before I could turn on the television or do an internet search and have a world of paranormal shows, websites, products, and information at my fingertips. This was a time before I was part of a fancy ghost hunting team and owned my own EMF detector.

Don't get me wrong, I absolutely love things just the way they are! But I also look back fondly on when, not that long ago, really, just the thrill of a good ghost story, whether found on the shelves of the local library or told around a dinner table by friends and family, captivated me and made me wonder about the world outside of people's everyday lives.

While I will touch on the history and folk- or ghostlore that are pertinent to each story, my main focus is to relate people's authentic personal experiences, in their own words where possible, in narrative and interview formats. My goal, while dispelling a few myths here and there, is to communicate the passion, drama, fear, thrills, and sometimes even the fun that not only the experiences, but the stories offer us.

This book should not be considered a thorough or extensive attempt to chronicle all the amazing haunted places in Maryland, but rather a glimpse into the variety and depth of encounters that regular people, as well as some seasoned ghost investigators, have had there.

The Resources & References section at the end of the book should provide further information and assist you in doing more research, reading, and adventuring on your own.

Those of us who have chosen to pursue the paranormal as a hobby, research field, or casual interest have all come to embrace it for different, very personal reasons. Hopefully, what's contained within these pages will add a little something to your collection and bring out even more of the mystery and magic of Maryland—or anywhere where spirits (and adventurers) may wander.

—Amelia Cotter

February 1, 2012
January 22, 2015

Part 1

Hauntings in Historic And Public Places

POINT LOOKOUT STATE PARK

Scotland, St. Mary's County

During the Civil War, the land that Point Lookout State Park currently occupies served as a Union Army fort, as well as prisoner of war camp and hospital for captured Confederates. More than 50,000 soldiers were imprisoned there in tents, and about 4,000 of them died.

Today the park is abuzz year-round with campers, hikers, swimmers, and fishers enjoying the surrounding Chesapeake Bay and Potomac River. But remnants of the Civil War and those who suffered remain, including the original Fort Lincoln, a four-sided earthen fort constructed for the defense of Point Lookout, and plenty of ghosts.

I took a trip to the park with one of my best friends, Jen, and a couple of our other good friends in the late summer of 2003, when few visitors were around and it was chilly enough to wear a coat at night. Each of us was (and still is) a history and paranormal enthusiast. We planned to spend the night in a cabin and explore the grounds, see the Point Lookout Light—the park's famous haunted lighthouse built in 1830—and go crabbing the next morning.

We were already pretty familiar with some of the ghost stories told about the park, although ghost hunting was not really our primary goal for the trip.

The lighthouse was surrounded by a fence and fully visible from the road, but not accessible. It is said to be haunted by a woman in blue who has been seen glowing in the upper windows of the house. Those who have lived there or have had access to the building have also reported disembodied voices, flying objects, and phantom lights in the windows.

In the park itself, sleeping campers at certain camping plots are awakened during the night by the sensation of someone hitting their feet, as if a Union soldier were still patrolling his prisoners and poking at them with the butt of his musket—just to check if the still ones are dead or only sleeping.

One of the most disturbing incidences happens to visitors as they drive along the road away from the park. They look into their rearview mirrors and see the eerie, solid images of Civil War soldiers marching or jogging in formation behind their car.

It was a long drive from our hometown of Bel Air in Harford County to the park, so when we arrived and got settled into our small cabin, we decided to take a brief nap before cooking out and exploring. It was around mid-afternoon.

Jen says that as she was drifting in and out of sleep, she could hear the distant sound of drumming. It was slow and rhythmic, and constant. She heard it as she fell asleep, and again as she woke up. Later, one of our other friends, Andrew, admitted that he had heard the drumming, too, after Jen asked us about it.

Fort Lincoln, one of Point Lookout State Park's many beautiful, well-preserved, historic, and haunted sites. *Photo courtesy of the author.*

We later learned that hearing this rhythmic drumming is another common paranormal experience in the park, and is perhaps the somber echo of Union drums assisting the soldiers in their drills or urging on laboring Confederates.

During our little nap, Jen also had another strange experience. She was sharing her bed with her boyfriend of the time. Andrew and I slept on bunk beds against the wall. At some point, Jen's boyfriend got up to go use the communal campground bathroom, just a short walk from the cabin. She said she was awake when this happened and aware that he had gotten up and left, and then heard the door to the cabin open and close again and felt him lie down next to her.

At this time, I woke up and asked her where her boyfriend was. Jen turned to see who was in the bed next to her...and found the space empty. He clearly hadn't yet returned.

Interestingly, this was the last of the paranormal activity that we experienced at Point Lookout, but the residue of the ghostly, almost sad beating of the drums stayed with us throughout the trip. That night, we grilled out and told stories, drove up to the lighthouse and waited to see the lady in blue (who did *not* appear for us), and explored Fort Lincoln with only flashlights and cameras to protect us, all without incident.

The only other thing that could be considered anywhere near frightening was baiting the crab traps on the next quiet, foggy morning...with live worms and raw chicken parts.

HELL HOUSE
Ellicott City, Howard County

Hell House, sometimes called "Creepy College," is a legendary Maryland haunt shrouded in myth and mystery. It is often confused with the nearby Patapsco Female Institute, which is an entirely different Ellicott City structure that is still well-maintained and even open for tours. The real name of Hell House was St. Mary's College of Maryland. It was a well-respected and nationally regarded seminary for men of the Roman Catholic Congregation of the Most Holy Redeemer, also known as The Redemptorists.

The school opened in 1868 and closed in 1972 due to a general decrease in enrollment. The school was later sold to the State of Maryland in 1987 and incorporated into Patapsco State Park. It was partially destroyed by fire in 1997, leaving a gaping hole in the upper part of the structure, which lent to its striking appearance at the top of the hill overlooking the Patapsco River near Ilchester Road.

All remnants of the building were officially torn down in February 2006, but a mysterious staircase near the train tracks at Hilltop Road still leads to the top of the hill where the college once stood.

Hell House got its chilling moniker from the numerous, intense and bloody legends circulating about what went on there both during and after its time as a religious institution. As teenagers, most of us were well-versed in the legends of Hell House: an insane priest had slaughtered several female students (this is likely due to the confusion with the Patapsco Female Institute), another priest hanged himself after the discovery of his illicit affair with a nun, and animals had been sacrificed as part of satanic rituals both before and after the school was abandoned.

Other popular stories circulated about what went on at Hell House after it was abandoned, including tales of séances, parties, and vandalism that certainly had some truth to them. Thrown in were the descriptions of the numerous discarded drug syringes and so much debris lining the property that it was difficult and dangerous to walk around up there. A mysterious dark pit was located in the central foundation of the main building. Deer would sometimes wander onto the property, fall into the empty outdoor pool, and die.

Ghost stories were frequently told about the shadow figures (human-shaped apparitions that appear in black or grey form) and mysterious lights that could be seen in the windows late at night. One young lady, Melissa, contacted me over Facebook with her Hell House story…

• • •

On a mild evening in October, Melissa and a group of her friends decided to check out Hell House after years of hearing about its nefarious reputation. It was dusk when they made their way up the aforementioned staircase, and dark by the time they hurried back down.

The staircase leading up to the place where Hell House once stood, near the train tracks at Hilltop Road, can still be climbed. *Photo courtesy of the author.*

The fact that Hell House was set on top of a hill and shrouded in woods already gave this group of friends a creepy feeling just walking up to it.

"As we made it to the top of the stairs," Melissa explained, "we had to twist and turn a couple of yards before we had a clear view of the building. We never actually made it to the building, because as we walked up, we looked up and saw something in the last window on the left of the top floor. It was a dark shadowy figure. Everyone in the group saw it."

The problem is that this particular part of the building had been destroyed by the fire, so only the façade of Hell House was still there. As Melissa says, "There was nothing left behind that particular wall for anyone to stand on, or climb up on and play tricks on people from. Our group had already seen enough and we hurried right back down the stairs to our cars."

• • •

Even more vivid than the bloody legends or tales of Hell House being haunted, were the stories always told about "a friend of a friend" who had encountered the caretaker of the property and his vicious dogs. The fire that had partially destroyed the building was alleged to have been started by a group of angry parents taking revenge on the caretaker after he shot and killed a trespassing teenager.

There actually was a caretaker of the property named Allen Rufus Hudson, who owned a number of dogs that would bark loudly enough to make what was probably a very intimidating sound echoing off the abandoned walls of the property. He was known to be a difficult and eccentric person, but he never killed anyone and was never the target of the 1997 fire.

I remember driving to Ellicott City at night with friends and seeing the old factory that sits at the bottom of the hill, the railroad tracks, and the looming silhouette of Hell House overlooking it all. I worked up the courage to visit Hell House twice: once at night when the graffiti and destruction from local thrill seekers actually did deter us from entering, and once during the day after it had been torn down and was just a pile of bricks and cement.

All that's left of St. Mary's College of Maryland, better known as "Hell House," which was officially torn down in February 2006. *Photo courtesy of the author.*

Whether the former residents of Hell House, living and dead alike, are as evil as this place's reputation suggests will never be known. It's possible Melissa and her friends simply glimpsed a spirit of a former student or teacher who was sticking around for not so interesting reasons. Or, if the rumors about séances and rituals are true, who knows what may have been—and may still be—lurking at the top of the hill where Hell House once stood.

THE INN AT DEEP CREEK LAKE

Oakland, Garrett County

The following incident was *almost* a personal experience. I was there, but fast asleep for most of it.

In August of 1996, I was on an ideal summer vacation with my parents at Deep Creek Lake in far Western Maryland, complete with hiking, a boat ride, bike rides along the C&O canal, and a white water rafting trip on the nearby Youghiogheny River.

Our hotel was built close to the lake's shore and at the time, it was a dated, dark, and oddly furnished Swiss-chalet style hotel called the Alpine Village Inn. Today, it goes by the more modern name of Inn at Deep Creek Lake and was fully renovated in 2010.

Tales circulated through the Inn about more than just the good area fishing spots and the local booming black bear population. The ghosts of Native Americans were said to haunt the inn grounds. Artifacts from the Cherokee, Shawnee, and Delaware Indians have been found near Deep Creek Lake, although members of the indigenous Mingo tribe mostly inhabited the area before the Europeans showed up.

The restaurant near the inn was allegedly haunted by the ghost of an Indian chief, who was seen strolling regally from room to room on an almost daily basis. The restaurant also operates under a new name today, so it's possible the renovations there and at the Inn have altered paranormal activity, and maybe even triggered more of it.

At the time, there was even a leaflet included in the restaurant's menu to educate, or warn, guests about the chief's regular appearances from the other side.

The first night we stayed at the Inn, we ate dinner at the Inn's restaurant. I had my eye out the whole time for any paranormal activity, ever hopeful that something extraordinary would happen, of course, within the hour and a half that *I* was there.

After a nice dinner, we returned to our room, ready for sleep after a long day of adventures.

I remember that after we got settled in and everything was quiet, I kept hearing the low murmur of men's voices talking in a language I didn't recognize. Even though we were in a two-story hotel with rooms on either side of us, the sounds seemed like they were right in the room with us and yet muffled at the same time. They didn't sound like voices coming through the wall from a television, and we also hadn't heard any other guests' conversations during our stay. The voices were clear and calm, and the discussion seemed to go on for hours until I fell asleep.

I woke up around 5 a.m. to a flurry of activity in the room. The first thing I saw was my mom sitting up in bed pointing toward the kitchen area of the room, which was on the other side of the wall from my bed.

My dad was in the kitchen murmuring obscenities while my mom asked what the hell was going on.

She was startled awake by what she described as "scratching noises" in the kitchen, then heard the door to the small hotel refrigerator blast open and all of its contents hit the floor. She woke my dad up and he jumped up to see what had happened. I must have woken up just seconds later.

Even though our room had no real hidden areas, open windows or doors, and the kitchen was basically the size of a large open closet, my mom was convinced that something was in the room with us.

I could hear my dad picking up the fallen soda cans and setting them on the counter. When my mom got up to help him I followed her.

As I peeked around the wall into the kitchen, I saw cans and water bottles all over the floor. (We were a thirsty bunch.) It was as if they were tossed with force. The suction on a refrigerator door would make it difficult for the door to just fall or fly open, and if it did, it doesn't seem like everything in the fridge would just fall out all over the place.

My dad was baffled and checked the main door to the room, the sliding glass door, and the windows, and everything was locked securely. The floors were all well sealed and it was obvious that no animals had gotten in.

My mom was entirely convinced, based on the noises she had heard, that something—or "someone large," as she kept saying—had to have done it.

I thought about this for the rest of our trip but we didn't speak of it again after that morning. We moved on to a different hotel after another night's stay at the Inn and it struck me as odd that we just kind of let the whole thing go.

Even as I interviewed my parents for this story and asked them about our stay at the hotel, they didn't seem to remember much about it until I started to describe my side of it again.

Of course, I also hadn't remembered that we took a boat ride while on the trip until they reminded me. Yet I remembered the restaurant menu in detail. Go figure.

JERICHO COVERED BRIDGE
Jerusalem, Harford County

The Jericho Covered Bridge is the last standing covered bridge in Harford County and one of few covered bridges left in Maryland. It's also a local legend and "rite of passage" site for young ghost hunters and explorers. A fully operational bridge on Jericho Road, street traffic travels back and forth on it daily through Jerusalem in Harford County and Kingsville in Baltimore County. The bridge is located over the Little Gunpowder Falls River in Gunpowder Falls State Park, and is part of the well-maintained Jerusalem Mill Village, thanks to the Friends of Jerusalem Mill organization.

Jerusalem Mill Village was once a Quaker settlement built around Jerusalem Mill, a grist mill that began operations in 1772. The "Gunshop," which is located behind the mill, was believed to be a musket production facility for the Maryland militia during the Revolutionary War.

The village was a thriving settlement until the mill ceased operations in 1961. Soon after it shut down, the State of Maryland purchased the property, and in 1985, the

Friends of Jerusalem Mill organization was formed to restore and maintain it.

Jericho Bridge itself was built in 1865 to provide an alternative method of transporting grain over the Little Gunpowder Falls instead of using Jerusalem Road, the main turnpike in the area at the time. The bridge has been listed in the National Register of Historic Places since September 1978.

There are numerous ghost stories associated with the bridge. Many are sad and, as one would expect, a few are hackneyed old tales. Covered bridges are often romanticized as iconic pieces of "Americana," so it's natural that they would also be excellent vehicles for tales about the darker side of life. Similar to the "Crybaby Bridge" legends that pervade many towns and counties across the U.S., sounds of a crying baby that was thrown into the river and drowned can be heard near the bridge at night, and the ghost of its despondent mother is seen searching the area for her lost child. People have actually reported seeing an adult female ghost in the area.

One interesting tale is that of a little girl who died on the bridge in a carriage fire. The details of the incident are lost to history. The bridge has undergone several renovations over the years, perhaps at one point due to a fire. The girl and her father were crossing the bridge when a lantern in the carriage fell over. It caught fire and the little girl died. The image of her face was eerily "burnt" into the bottom of the bridge and could be viewed from beneath it for years before more recent renovations covered it up. Her ghost allegedly still haunts the bridge.

Another version of this story places it in a more modern context and states that the girl was riding in a truck with her father when a kerosene lamp fell over and started the fire.

The most frequently experienced and disturbing piece of ghostlore, however, is that of the hanging slaves. According to many sources, a number of slaves were hanged from the rafters of the bridge as a political statement during the Civil War, when residents of the state of Maryland were split between allegiance to the North and South. The bridge was built in 1865, as the war was ending, so this can't be entirely true. However, it is possible that lynchings subsequently occurred at the bridge.

According to local legend, if you pull your car onto the bridge at night, turn off the engine and kill the lights, wait to the count of three, then start the car and hit the brakes, the red glow from the brake lights will illuminate the silhouettes of hanging bodies.

Not everyone has to go to such great lengths to see the hanging bodies, however. Sometimes these eerie figures and sad reminders of Maryland's past reveal themselves without the necessity of a car engine ritual. Sometimes they are not even seen, but felt, in the form of thudding footsteps on windshields, and white filmy foot- and handprints are found smeared across the tops of cars later.

I interviewed two people about Jericho Bridge, my friend Jen who has contributed multiple stories to this book, and paranormal investigator Samantha Kelley, founder of Kelleyano Researchers and Investigators of the Paranormal (K.R.I.P.). Both have vivid recollections of their run-ins with the paranormal at this quiet, unassuming place, and Samantha later sent me some very compelling photos that her team took during their investigations there…

•   •   •

Interview with Jen

Me: Do you remember when you first visited the bridge?

Jen: We went there many times, but the first time we had anything happen was in high school sometime. There was a group of about ten of us. It was someone's birthday. We had parked in the State Park lot on Jerusalem Road and walked over to the bridge.

Me: What time of year was it? Were you worried about getting caught by park rangers?

Jen: It was early spring and foggy and chilly out. And yes, I remember that we were standing around trying to be quiet and trying not to get caught.

Me: What happened next?

Jen: As a car came from the Kingsville side of the bridge, it saw us and slowed down, and as it was about to pass, we saw its headlights shine on the inside of the bridge. Several of us very clearly saw the shadow of a hanging person on the inside of the bridge. A couple of us shouted out at the same time. Everyone described seeing the same thing.

Me: What other experiences did you have there?

Jen: Well, I remember the other thing that happened, which was worse. It was hot out. We were coming back from a trip to Gettysburg. It may have been the summer we graduated high school or the one before, so 2003 or 2002, I don't remember.

The windows were down and we heard a thud on the roof. We rolled up the windows—they were the kind you had to hand crank—and I turned the car around and we sped out of there! Then we went to a lit parking lot, I think it was a gas station, just to get a soda and stop for a minute. I looked at the back window and in the light, saw a giant white handprint.

Both the guys with us got out and put their hands up to the print. It was almost twice the size of their hands and the fingers were really long. The print was very clear, you could even see the wrinkles of the fingertips.

Me: I remember hearing other stories later, similar to that— footprints and hand prints appearing on cars in this white residue substance. What happened to the print?

Jen: It was gone the next day and we couldn't get a good photo of it in the dark. I drive that road sometimes but I don't stop on the bridge anymore. The park rangers are also more careful than they used to be and it's hard to park or stop there at all.

•   •   •

Interview with Samantha Kelley of K.R.I.P.

Me: Tell me about your team.

Samantha: K.R.I.P. was founded in 2011 and we are a family-started paranormal team in Maryland. I am the founder and lead investigator, Shannon and Brianna are co-founders and investigators, Paula is an investigator and case manager, and Matt is an investigator and evidence analyzer. Our mission is to uncover evidence of the paranormal, as well as help people understand and become comfortable with it. From our experiences, we have grown to have an appreciation for the other side and want to help people understand and not fear it.

Me: You and your team are very familiar with the Jericho Covered Bridge. What particular legends have you heard regarding the bridge?

Samantha: Legend has it that several lynchings occurred at the bridge after the Civil War, in which the captured people were hung from the upper rafters, sometimes many at a time. If you stop your car on the narrow bridge late at night, and look in your rear view mirrors, the image of a swinging body can be seen. There have also been stories of a little girl that was killed there by accident in a fire.

Me: What paranormal experiences have you had there?

Samantha: Our team's investigations of the bridge took place on four different nights in July, the first two were two nights in a row, the third was about a week after that, and the fourth was a week after that. It was all around 10 p.m. to midnight on pretty clear, warm nights. The last one was during a full moon.

On our first trip, we decided to do a preliminary investigation of the area the night before the main investigation.

We decided just to drive through really quick since it was on the way to our house. We drove through and didn't see anything, but we did get a creepy feeling. As we were driving away we noticed this abandoned building up the street a few feet. I decided to get our camera out and take some pictures of the house to show the team member who wasn't with us.

When we got home, Paula noticed a weird spot on one of our pictures. I pulled it up on the computer and we found that we had captured what looked like a full apparition of a little girl wearing a white dress. After checking other pictures, we concluded that it was not a natural occurrence since it did not appear in any of the other pictures. This made us extremely excited for the next night's investigation.

The apparition of a little girl caught with a digital camera during K.R.I.P.'s first investigation of the Jericho Covered Bridge and surrounding area. Circle in the photo added by K.R.I.P. *Photo courtesy of Samantha Kelley.*

The next night we went back and Matt and I decided to do an EVP session [Electronic Voice Phenomena: capturing spirit voices on an electronic device]. During this EVP session I felt extremely uneasy, like someone was watching me. Shannon and Brianna were taking pictures and video.

We told Paula, Shannon, and Brianna to drive the car away and then come back to get us in 10 minutes so I could do an EVP session and Matt could film. During the session we heard what sounded like rocks being thrown. When Paula drove the car back I asked for the camera to take some more pictures. While I was doing this, Paula, Shannon, and Brianna were in the car, and the car started shaking while it was in park and it felt like it was moving forward.

Then we drove up to the abandoned building and I took some more pictures, one in the exact spot where we caught the girl to prove she wasn't a natural occurrence. We took everything home to review the evidence. What we found next was shocking.

In one of the pictures Shannon took of the rafters we saw what looked like legs and feet hanging down, but they were curled up slightly. Matt, a former City Firefighter and EMT, said it almost looked as if rigor mortis had set in, because the legs would naturally curl in, like the person had been hanging up there for a while.

I then told him that I had heard the bodies *had been* left hanging for a while, which was something I left out in the briefing of the stories to him. We also had a picture of the exact same area where you can see that the apparition of legs and feet are not there.

In our third investigation we didn't get as much tangible proof as we did personal experiences. Shannon, Brianna, Matt, and I were doing an EVP session and I kept hearing laughter and whispering. Unfortunately the river underneath the bridge was a lot louder that night because of rain the night before, so there was more water and it muffled our EVP sessions, and basically ruined any evidence we would have had.

The digital photo above shows an unexplained anomaly in the rafters of Jericho Covered Bridge, captured by K.R.I.P. on their second investigation there. They believe it is the apparition of a person who was hanged or lynched on the bridge. The digital photo on the next page, taken immediately after and with the camera's flash on, shows the same spot without any objects present that may have created the anomaly. Text and white circles in the photos added by K.R.I.P. *Photos courtesy of Samantha Kelley.*

Finally, on our fourth investigation we did an EVP session. At one point Matt says, "I want to see you do something...show us you're here. Touch one of the girls."

After he says that you hear a disembodied voice whisper, "I can't." This was outstanding because it told us there are two kinds of spirits there, one who is obviously intelligent and responding to our questions, and then the residual apparitions of the hanging men.

Me: What amazing evidence and experiences! How have they affected you and your group?

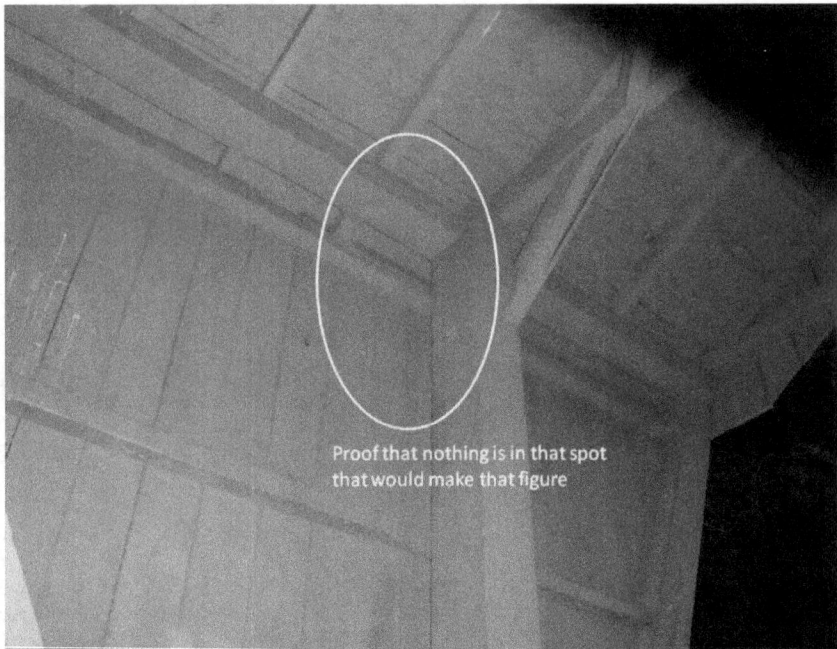

Proof that nothing is in that spot that would make that figure

Samantha: Our skeptic, Matt, who doesn't really believe in many of the things we find, really agrees that there are ghosts there. It's made me more passionate about finding evidence of the paranormal, proving to people that there is something after death, and finding the reasons why these spirits stay behind.

SCHIFFERSTADT MUSEUM
Frederick, Frederick County

The Schifferstadt Architectural Museum is an historic treasure that can be found on Rosemont Avenue, near the Hood College exit off of I-70. Built in 1758, it is one of the finest examples of colonial German architecture in the country, and boasts many of its original architectural features, including a large stone furnace inscribed in German with the biblical phrase, "For where your treasure is, there your heart will be also."

It is operated by the Frederick County Landmarks Foundation. Open to the public at certain times for tours and living history demonstrations, the Schifferstadt is dependent entirely on volunteer power, donations, and grants.

The original stone house was built by Josef Bruner, one of the many German immigrants who settled the Maryland and Pennsylvania areas. He traveled from his hometown of Schifferstadt, Germany to establish a home in what was at the time considered frontier land and a crossroads of battle during the French and Indian War.

The museum is allegedly haunted by several ghosts, including his. The house has seen numerous owners, occupants, and caretakers over the centuries, but the main spirits encountered are a male, a female, and a child that all seem to date from the late eighteenth and early nineteenth centuries. The little boy spirit is mostly seen in the attic, the female spirit in the kitchen area, and the male apparition in the gift shop on the first floor.

Volunteers and staff have also reported hearing disembodied voices echoing through the house (speaking in German, of course), footsteps, phantom doors slamming, and even hammering and construction sounds.

I did an internship at the Schifferstadt during two semesters in college as a freshman and into my sophomore year. I had a rather interesting experience while working up in the office alone on a crisp fall day. The inside door of the gift shop that leads to the upstairs is equipped with a set of jingle bells that prevents visitors from accidentally going up to an office area where they aren't allowed.

The museum was closed and I was by myself, working on the computer in the office. Sometimes other volunteers or an employee with a set of keys would stop by to drop something off or perform some other task for the museum. Without really thinking about it, I heard the door from the gift shop to the upstairs open and the bells start to jingle. I figured someone was coming up and I just hadn't heard the main front door open. Then I heard several heavy footsteps coming up the stairs.

At some point, they just stopped. I stopped typing and looked up, wondering why the person wasn't saying anything and had stopped halfway up the stairs. I had the distinct impression that there was a man there, and got up from my desk to walk over and see who he was. Of course, I saw no one, and the gift shop door was still closed.

I quietly returned to my desk, thoroughly weirded out, and resumed working.

There were a few other occasions when I remember being alone and getting a serious case of the creeps, suddenly and out of nowhere. My solution was usually to pretend I didn't notice anything and just keep working until the odd sensation would fade away.

The Schifferstadt is an otherwise friendly and inviting place, and the spirits are known to be warm and not scary. Perhaps Josef Brunner just likes to stop by every once in a while and see who is looking after his historic home.

THE BOY ON ST. MARY'S CHURCH ROAD

Bel Air, Harford County

On the surface, Bel Air is a town that doesn't seem to have a whole lot going on. It's pretty much a typical suburb, with a small historic main street area and plenty of sprawling strip malls and shopping centers. From a fine selection of brand-new cookie-cutter houses to a delightful variety of chain restaurants and home improvement stores, Bel Air offers up everything the perfect American family needs—never mind its dark past, filled with things that go on behind closed doors and the ghosts they create.

My friend Jen, who has shared several of her paranormal encounters for this book, came face to spectral face with evidence of the dark undercurrents of suburban life late one night along St. Mary's Church Road near Abingdon.

She was driving home with a friend, approaching St. Mary's from Laurel Bush Road. It was very late and they didn't expect to see anyone out. As they turned onto St.

Mary's, their headlights panned across an empty abandoned house.

There, standing near the edge of the road in front of the house, was a young boy about 12 or 13 years old. He was staring off into the distance, almost like he was in a daze. As they went by, he didn't move or react to the car or its bright headlights.

In fact, he didn't seem to notice them at all. According to Jen, "If you were waiting for someone, you'd look at the car passing. He didn't. He also looked like he was covered in blood and very dirty. His clothes were a mess."

Jen and her friend were immediately horrified, but when they turned to look back at him they didn't see him anymore. They stopped their car in the middle of the road and looked out the back window behind them, but were so unnerved they decided not to drive back and to just keep going.

Jen still lives in the area, and recalls that the house the boy was standing near had been empty for a while. Jen learned after the incident that the house had a hard time selling because potential buyers felt uncomfortable and scared by it.

Her mother-in-law had gone to look at the house with a real estate agent, well before the incident, and had a similar visceral reaction. She later heard what sounded much like an urban legend about the house, symbolic of suburban unrest: that a murder-suicide had occurred in the house, involving a father who shot his son and then himself. Whether this is true or not, Jen *had* seen a blood-covered boy by the side of the road that night.

The house was never sold and was finally donated to the Abingdon Fire Department a few years after Jen's encounter. Jen and her family accompanied her father-in-law, a volunteer fireman, to watch it burn down. She was reminded of her disturbing experience that night, and hopes the boy has finally found peace.

Jen's daughter stands in front of the abandoned house on St. Mary's Road, on the day the house was burned down by the Abingdon Fire Department, in the approximate spot where Jen had seen the apparition of a young boy. *Photo courtesy of Jarid Kranz.*

INTERVIEW WITH JENNIFER SHAPE OF CECIL AND BEYOND PARANORMAL
Elkton, Cecil County

Jennifer and Robert Shape are the founders of the ghost investigation team Cecil and Beyond Paranormal. Jennifer was eager to tell me about her team, their philosophy, their experiences with Cecil County haunts, and their yearly fundraiser at the Historic Elk Landing in Elkton.

The tract of land now known as Elk Landing has been in use since the early 1600s, when it was a Swedish and Finnish trading post. It was also an important port during the War of 1812. The main manor at Elk Landing, also known as Hollingsworth Manor, was built in 1747. Now, the property is maintained by the Historic Elk Landing Foundation.

Cecil and Beyond have worked in tandem with the Foundation for the past three years to produce a ghost hunting event, with all proceeds benefiting Elk Landing. Jennifer and her team are out to show by example that many ghost hunting teams prefer to give back to their communities and help preserve historic places rather than desecrate them...

• • •

Me: Tell me about your team.

Jennifer: We are located in Cecil County. We have done a lot of investigations in Cecil County, both business and residential. Robert and I are the founders, and our junior founder is Joshua Shape, our son.

Some of our best evidence is from private cases, which we can't talk about, but we have done other cases, many that have given us shadow figures.

Me: Can you tell me more about those cases?

Jennifer: One of them is the Historical Society of Cecil County, located in Elkton. Marsha was investigating the first floor and doing an EVP session there while holding the digital camcorder. She was panning around with the camcorder around the book section. She felt like she saw something move and it was confirmed while going over the evidence. You can see it on our website.

Another case we have done many times, at a place very close to our hearts, is the Historic Elk Landing. On our first investigation there, we discovered a woman and child ghost in the main manor, and a not so nice male ghost in the stone house. He isn't there to hurt anyone, but doesn't like anyone in his space. He's told us many times to "get out." We find that a lot in our cases.

Me: I take it you've conducted several investigations at Elk Landing?

Jennifer: Yes. We did another investigation there to confirm the evidence we had gotten from that first one. We were very happy that the spirits were willing to talk with us. We find that going into an investigation and asking for permission from the spirits to be there is always a plus, and we always let the spirits know we are there to hear their story.

Me: Is this how the idea for the fundraiser came about?

Jennifer: Yes. After the second investigation at Elk Landing we proposed to the Board of the Historic Elk Landing Foundation that we do a public ghost hunt as a fundraiser for them. It was a huge success! We had about 200 people show up in the cold and rain to "be a ghost hunter for a night." The public was able to use our equipment and go through both the main manor and the stone house. The whole tour lasted about one hour per group, and the public was very happy to do something that they have only seen on television.

We were asked back by Elk Landing to do a second year. That year we brought in over 200 people, this time giving a history of the house and grounds, along with the ghost hunt in the manor and stone house.

We just need to work on solving the noise contamination problem for this year's (2011) ghost hunt. There were so many people at the last event that all the audio evidence was ruined. We only accept recordings that are clear. We have been asked to do two nights this time, to try to spread out the crowds and to possibly give everyone even more time on the tours.

Me: It sounds like a great event for a great cause!

Jennifer: We do this for the benefit of the Historic Elk Landing Foundation. We have such a love and respect for that place, for the history, and for the spirits that reside there. We want the public to learn and to help preserve our historic locations. This is our history on the line, and if places like Elk Landing are forgotten then they are subject to developers and lost forever.

THE DR. SAMUEL A. MUDD HOUSE
Waldorf, Charles County

Dr. Samuel Mudd is rather infamously known as a conspirator in the assassination of President Abraham Lincoln in 1865. He was an acquaintance of John Wilkes Booth, and historians speculate both accusatorily and sympathetically about their relationship and just how involved in the conspiracy Dr. Mudd actually was.

As a medical doctor, Mudd took Booth into his home early in the morning after Lincoln's assassination to set his broken leg. To put it simply, Mudd was not quick to report this to police. He was eventually convicted of conspiracy and spent several years in prison until he was pardoned by President Andrew Johnson in 1869. He then returned to his home, continued his medical practice, and maintained the family farm until his death in 1883. His house is now open to the public at certain times and is run on donations and volunteer power by the Dr. Samuel A. Mudd Society.

Inspired Ghost Tracking (I.G.T.) is a Maryland-based team that performs regular home and business investigations. I.G.T. member Ronda Dixon has performed several investigations at the Mudd House with some of her teammates. During our interview, she filled me in on her experiences there and shared with me one of the most impressive apparition photos I have ever seen, which she took in the house after feeling like someone was following her down the stairs. Ronda, along with I.G.T. founder Margaret Perry Ehrlich, the photo, and their story were featured on Episode 59 of *My Ghost Story* in 2013, but they shared it all with me for *Maryland Ghosts* first…

•   •   •

Me: Where exactly is the Mudd House and can you tell me a bit about the site?

Ronda: Dr. Mudd's house and farm are in the Southern part of Maryland, located at 3725 Dr. Samuel Mudd Road in Waldorf, Maryland. When you first arrive at the farm, you will see what looks like a typical farmhouse with barns and other outer buildings. A long horse-shoe shaped road leads you to the back of the house. That is now the entrance to the gift shop and also to the home.

Me: Tell me about some of the experiences you've had there.

Ronda: On one of my visits, while I was investigating the back yard and walking back toward the house, I was touched on my back. At first I thought I had bumped into something, but upon looking around I found that I was in the middle of the yard with nothing around me. Several of my pictures captured bright orbs and mists.

Entering the house you are welcomed into a dining room with a large table set for dinner. The living room is filled with antique furniture and family heirlooms, along with the actual couch where Dr. Mudd placed Booth to rest after his arrival. This also happens to be the place where I first started having cold chills there. Mists and orbs have also been captured in this area.

A small bedroom is also located on the first floor of the home. This is where the doctor slept so he could hear if anyone would come knocking on his door in the middle of the night seeking medical attention, which is exactly what Booth did.

The second floor has two bedrooms and also Dr. Mudd's office. The upper bedroom toward the front of the house is where John Wilkes Booth stayed and rested for a day. I figured that this was a great place to set up my video camera while I investigated the rest of the rooms. When I returned later to get the camera, I discovered that my camera had not recorded a thing, as someone had turned it off.

Me: How did you capture that amazing photo?

Ronda: This was on that same visit. As I was heading back downstairs from getting my video camera, I continued to take pictures with my regular digital camera. Just as I was taking this picture of the hallway mirror, I felt that someone or something had come down the stairs behind me. Not wanting to jump to conclusions, I wanted to wait until I arrived back home to check all my pictures.

Arriving home late, I actually waited until morning to place my pictures on my computer. After reviewing most of the evidence, some with orbs and some with misty shapes, I finally got to this mirror picture.

There in the mirror was a man actually walking down the stairs. He looks like an older man with dark hair, slightly hunched over, maybe wearing glasses, and with something around his neck, like a collar or a scarf. I was amazed. Not only was I being followed down the stairs as I had thought, but I couldn't believe what I was seeing. Could it be the ghost of Dr. Samuel Mudd, coming back to reclaim his innocence?

An apparition caught with a digital camera during an investigation of the Dr. Samuel Mudd House. The photo on the next page was cropped and enlarged for a closer view. *Photos courtesy of Ronda Dixon.*

• • •

I got a chance to visit the Mudd House in late 2014 and learned that the home has always remained in the Mudd family. As a result of the love Dr. Mudd and his family had for each other, and the fact that generations of the Mudd family have taken excellent care of the place and held on to many of the family's original treasures, I felt an immense sense of love and warmth pervading the entire home.

Upon seeing various Dr. Mudd portraits hanging throughout the house, I am not convinced he is the same man in the apparition photo. But I do wonder if the man in the photo is a Mudd descendant, checking in on the home and its visitors from time to time. Either way, a fascinating and wonderful capture.

THE PRY HOUSE FIELD HOSPITAL MUSEUM
Sharpsburg, Washington County

In September 1862, the hilltop farmhouse owned by the Phillip Pry family in Sharpsburg was transformed into Union General George McClellan's U.S. Army headquarters. This was shortly before the single bloodiest day in U.S. history—the Battle of Antietam on September 17—the first major battle of the Civil War on Northern soil, which claimed over 23,000 lives.

Immediately after the battle, the house and the surrounding barn and property were turned into a field hospital where the wounded were treated. Union Medical Director Dr. Jonathan Letterman practiced medicine and surgical techniques that, contrary to modern beliefs about medical care at the time, are considered to be the foundation of modern military medicine and triage care.

General Joseph Hooker was among the wounded treated at the Pry House, along with General Israel Richardson, who was not seriously hurt in the battle but taken into the house to receive care. Richardson stayed there for the next several months, his wife coming from their home state of Michigan to be by his side, as his condition deteriorated and he came down with pneumonia. He eventually died in the home after about six months.

The house continued to be a private residence for many years until it was taken over by the National Park Service and became a stop along driving tours of the Antietam National Battlefield. It even housed Park Service workers for a short time, but for the most part stood empty until it was opened by the National Museum of Civil War Medicine as the Pry House Field Hospital Museum in 2005.

The first floor is open to the public for part of the year with artifacts and exhibits including lifelike mannequins recreating the scene of an operating table. Stories circulate about the house's resident ghost in charge—not, surprisingly, one of the Pry's or General Richardson—but Richardson's wife, Fannie, affectionately known to everyone simply as "Mrs. Richardson."

A lot of paranormal activity has been experienced by Park Service and Museum employees, volunteers, and visitors. People have reported multiple run-ins with Mrs. Richardson, as well as with other spirits. I worked at the Pry House as a Visitor Services Representative over the course of several summers while in college and heard a number of interesting stories.

The most famous story told revolves around the fire that happened in the house in 1976 while it was still a private residence. There are two versions of this subsequent Mrs. Richardson sighting. The first one states that after the family safely got out of the burning home, firefighters saw a woman looking out of one of the second floor windows and ran inside to save her. When they got inside, they realized that the floor the woman would have been standing on had already collapsed.

The other version of this story suggests that the sighting happened later, during the house's restoration. Workers went into the house to search for a woman they had seen in the same upstairs window, only to discover that there was no floor up there for her to stand on.

Either way, the second floor was completely rebuilt, and people continue to spot Mrs. Richardson gazing out of one of the upper windows of the home, from the room where her husband stayed before he died.

She, or another female ghost, has also been seen in other parts of the house. It is not uncommon for a docent or volunteer to come to work at the Pry House in period clothing, and on various occasions, visitors have seen a woman in Victorian dress around the house. When they ask who the reenactor on site is, they are informed by employees that there is no such volunteer or docent that day.

The Pry House was still being renovated for the first several months after being opened as a museum, and renovations to a home or building can often trigger or cause an increase in paranormal activity. During this time, some people were even approached by Mrs. Richardson, up close and personal. My friend and former coworker, Tina, remembers hearing about the following frightening encounters with her…

• • •

Once, a staff member's son was in the main office on the second floor, across the hall from the room where General Richardson died. The staff member later recounted to me that the boy was doing his homework or some other project and looked up and saw "an angry woman" staring at him from the doorway. Then she disappeared.

I was actually in the house at the time, working downstairs, and I remember the boy flying down the stairs and out the back door. He jumped into his father's car, which was parked nearby, and refused to go back into the house. In fact, I don't think his father succeeded in getting him out of the car the rest of the day. This boy wasn't faking it, he was *really* upset.

Only a few days earlier, a volunteer was helping paint the house. He told me that he'd gone into the pantry in the kitchen for some supplies and heard, next to his right shoulder, a woman's voice whispering, "Get out." His description of the voice was that it was "very angry."

The Pry House Field Hospital Museum, site of General George McClellan's Union headquarters during the Battle of Antietam. After the battle, the home, barn, and grounds were used as a field hospital where numerous soldiers were treated for their wounds. *Photo courtesy of the author.*

• • •

As stated, not all paranormal experiences at the Pry House are with the lovely Mrs. Richardson. Tina also told me about her daily checks of the upstairs and the attic...

When I'd first get there on my mornings and I went up to open the door to the attic, every once in a while a strong smell of pancakes and syrup would blast out. The first time this happened, I thought that somebody else on the staff had actually had a pancake dinner the night before somewhere on the second floor, and the aroma hadn't dissipated yet.

Other days there would be no smell, just the old dusty normal attic smell. The first time I took my son there, I took him up to the attic, deliberately not having told him anything, and as soon as we opened the door he said, "Wow! Pancakes!"

• • •

Those familiar with my first book, *This House: The True Story of a Girl and a Ghost*, will remember the sequence in the first chapter when the latch to the locked, unused door in the kitchen mysteriously lifts itself one afternoon in spite of being very heavy. This, too, happened at the Pry House, during the summer I decided to get serious about writing ghost stories!

That latch lifting itself made a noise loud enough for my coworker and me, alone at the time in both the house and on the property, to go investigate. When we tried to move the latch back into place, we couldn't, not even with all the effort of both hands and leaning our full weight into the door. Something powerful had lifted that latch.

I had one other encounter there during a previous summer. I was closing up at the end of the day and setting the alarm, with my coworker waiting for me outside. As I was dialing in the code, I heard the loud voice of a man with a slight southern drawl echoing down the front hallway, just 15 feet in front of me. It was as if he were asking a question, but it was so abrupt I didn't catch the words.

I just stared and blinked in shock, and then my coworker asked me what was taking so long. I suddenly remembered that I had just a few seconds to get out before the alarm would go off when I opened the door. When I got outside I didn't tell her what happened. I asked if she was talking to anyone or if anyone was around. There was no one there and she obviously hadn't heard or noticed anything. The parking lot was empty.

The incident surprised me, but I wasn't really scared. The voice was so real, and so *ordinary*. It didn't really hit me until I was on the road that it must have been a ghost. It was rather fascinating, actually, to hear a voice from the past.

THE NATIONAL MUSEUM OF CIVIL WAR MEDICINE
Frederick, Frederick County

A building that houses a vast collection of artifacts and life-like mannequins performing medical demonstrations from the Civil War, conveying both the physical and emotional suffering of hundreds of thousands of people, is bound to be haunted.

The National Museum of Civil War Medicine (NMCWM), founded in 1990, brings the history of medical advancements of the Civil War to life and breaks down historical stereotypes about clumsy surgeons and careless treatments. Using eerily realistic mannequins and interactive audio and video, the museum chronicles, in graphic and personal detail, the nature of camp and hospital life, and the rapid innovations in military medicine that are still in use today.

The museum is home to the last intact Confederate surgical tent, as well as an original operating table, prosthetic limbs, and numerous other fascinating pieces of

Civil War history that tell the story of what happened after the battles were over.

The three-story facility in downtown Frederick was originally a furniture store owned by James Whitehill in 1832. Later, during the Civil War, Whitehill capitalized on the large number of dead soldiers being moved through Frederick by turning the building into an undertaking business, as Frederick was a large city at the time and centrally located along transportation routes. There was a great demand for coffins and headstones, and often, the home towns and states of the dead were too far for them to be carried the entire way. Whitehill created a one-stop shop for coffins, headstones, and the preparation of bodies on site.

Rumors still circulate that Whitehill was a corrupt man who would steal back headstones he had manufactured, refinish them, and resell them to new patrons. He sold the business to Clarence Carty after the Civil War ended. According to legend, Whitehill's illicit activities were discovered and he was run out of town.

With such an intense history, and layers of artifacts and personal items that spirits could remain attached to, it is no wonder the museum is known to be one of the most haunted places in Frederick.

During my sophomore year in college, I started to volunteer at the museum and later worked as a Visitor Services Representative (VSR) there. In addition to being afraid of the mannequins and getting generally strange vibes in certain areas of the building, I once witnessed a row of books fall off a shelf in the gift shop. They were stacked one behind the other with their covers facing outward, so that when they fell off one by one, the effect was like watching someone flip the pages of a book.

I also recall that people would faint in the same area over and over, near the surgery exhibit on the first floor. The subject matter could certainly get gruesome in various parts of the museum, and it seemed like more than coincidence that people would suddenly feel sick or collapse in that particular spot.

But my experiences don't nearly match up to what happened to some of my former coworkers. It was not uncommon to pass the time swapping ghost stories, and some of the employees were more than happy to talk to me about their paranormal run-ins with the numerous ghosts rumored to haunt the building…

• • •

The third floor is said to be the most haunted area of the building. Not part of the exhibitions, it houses the museum's administrative offices. My former coworker, Robby, was instructed to go up there one day while the offices were closed and check on something. After he went up and completed the task, he got on the passenger elevator to go back down. Just as the doors were closing, he heard voices. Curious, he quickly pushed the "door open" button to listen closer. He wasn't sure if the sound of voices was a trick of the elevator doors closing.

As he continued to listen, he again heard what sounded like the voices of two men holding a conversation in a back office. The voices were clear but low and the words were indistinct. He had just been back near that office and hadn't seen anyone. Holding the elevator door open with one hand, he turned the corner to listen even closer. He could *still* hear the voices, and they continued, not seeming to notice him, until he felt the overwhelming urge to leave.

• • •

Another former VSR, Kierstin, told me even more frightening stories about working at the museum...

I was working with Gwen, a fellow VSR. We were sitting at the front desk in the main lobby area one afternoon. The museum was mostly empty. Out of nowhere, we both heard a muffled blood curdling scream. It was comparable to the kind of screams you hear in horror movies. We searched the building and even stepped outside, but couldn't find a source for the scream. The sound was close to us but muffled. We were convinced that it had come from the *inside* of the building.

Another time, I was sitting at the front desk and heard giggling. I looked around and no one was there. The temperature dropped suddenly. It got really cold and the door to the desk swung open about three inches.

Yet another time, I was sitting at the front desk with Gwen and Robby when the temperature suddenly dropped again. Then, what looked like a small cloud of smoke passed right by my face.

Once, I was alone on the third floor and the door to the emergency stairwell slammed even though I had propped it open with a very heavy box.

I also remember hearing voices in the exhibits on the second floor, when no one else was up there. After a while, I refused to go up to the second floor alone. There were also the occasional books falling off of shelves in the gift shop on the first floor. I always felt that I was being watched there.

All of these events scared the hell out of me at the time! I would get goose bumps constantly and was always very uncomfortable.

•   •   •

Our coworker Gwen also weighed in on her experiences, including her side of the "blood curdling scream" incident…

While I was working as a VSR at the museum, I worked Saturdays and Sundays with Kierstin. One day, there were a few people back in the exhibits, but for the most part it was pretty quiet. We were working on our crossword puzzles when we heard a blood curdling scream from inside the museum. I checked the security cameras and the exhibits and no one had heard or noticed anything. We ran outside and no one had heard anything out there either. We were never able to pinpoint the source of that scream.

On another occasion, I was checking the security monitor behind the front desk. It would display, in real time, every room that a security camera was watching. The camera placed in the exhibit with the hospital flag was pointed at a wall of flip panels that had photos on one side and information on the other. I watched as all of the panels on the wall slowly opened by themselves and then closed again.

Many of the volunteers at the museum would like to wear period clothing when they gave tours. One volunteer docent often wore full black mourning attire. One day, the development officer at the time saw a woman wearing black mourning attire pass by her in one of the exhibits. She called out, "Good morning, Barbara!" The woman then walked through a wall and vanished.

The collections manager at the time had a seven year-old son who he would often bring to work with him. One day, a few staff members were chatting in the kitchen on the third floor and heard him and his son come up the stairs and walk down the hall.

One of the staff members peeked around the corner and actually saw a man and child walking down the hall. Naturally, she thought it was them. About ten minutes later, she called out to them but they didn't answer. A few minutes after that, the real collections manager stepped off the elevator—his son wasn't with him and he hadn't been upstairs or in his office yet that morning.

•   •   •

There were many occasions when I was alone in parts of the building before or after hours, and I vividly remember scurrying as fast as I could through dark exhibits and down long, empty corridors. I loved the museum and my time working there, and I never felt unwelcome, but there was a constant, overwhelming sense that "something" else was there.

Sometimes the simple presence of spirit energy causes us to have a natural instinctual reaction of fear, when in fact the spirits mean no harm. Most of the time the spirits just *are*, and in the case of the National Museum of Civil War Medicine, they maintain quite a strong presence that is sure to be felt by all who enter.

Part 2

HAUNTED HOUSES AND PRIVATE RESIDENCES

A HAUNTING ON SOUTH MOUNTAIN

Middletown, Frederick County

South Mountain is a 70-mile long extension of the Blue Ridge Mountains and is part of the greater Appalachian Mountain Range. It is home to the small, rural towns of Middletown and nearby Boonsboro and Burkittsville. The area is as rich in history as it is in fascinating local legends and lore that date back several centuries.

The mountain was the site of the Civil War's Battle of South Mountain, also called the Battle of Boonsboro Gap, which occurred at Crampton's, Fox, and Turner's Gaps on September 14, 1862—just three days before the Battle of Antietam over the mountain in Sharpsburg.

Ghostlore of the area includes "Spook Hill" in Burkittsville, an anti-gravity spot along the road winding up the mountain. This phenomenon, or perhaps optical illusion, causes cars to roll uphill when they are stopped and placed in neutral in one particular spot. Legend says that the cars are being pushed by the spirits of Civil War soldiers who believe the vehicles are cannons. If you do this experiment at midnight, you can even hear the sound of the soldiers marching behind your car.

The non-Civil War related ghost of the White Lady is a woman seen wearing a long, flowing white or glowing blue dress. She wanders the mountain near Middletown and in some folktales is known as a banshee that omens bad fortune.

It's hard to talk about the supernatural in connection with South Mountain and its surrounding areas without taking a moment to mention its most illustrious supernatural residents: the Snarly Yow, Dwayyo, and Snallygaster.

The Snarly Yow is a black dog-like creature, often seen with red eyes or a gaping red mouth. It confronts travelers along the road in Middletown and sometimes even chases cars. Reported encounters with the creature date back almost a century.

The Dwayyo is a werewolf-like creature that is not related to the Snarly Yow. The Dwayyo is considered by some to be a cryptid—a plausible member of the animal kingdom whose existence has not yet been proven by mainstream science. It walks bi-pedally and appears in half-man, half-wolf form. The legend of the Dwayyo originated in Middletown and developed sometime during the mid- to late 1700s when the first European settlers on South Mountain probably encountered large predatory animals such as black bears and coyotes. Sightings of the Dwayyo have been reported up through the twentieth century.

Lastly, the Snallygaster also traces its origins to the colonial days of the mountain, in nearby Braddock Heights to the east of Middletown, where early German settlers reported encountering a "schneller Geist," or quick spirit, that would cause mischief on their farms and eat their livestock. The beast is said to resemble a large, flying half-bird, half-reptile with tentacles. There are still barns in the area with paintings of the creature on the side of them, either to ward them off or simply to celebrate this home-grown legend.

With such a plethora of paranormal inhabitants and locations in a small area, nestled up to the side of a mountain, why, who *wouldn't* want to live in Middletown? When I contacted my friend and former college housemate Kim about the German House at Hood College, she was eager to share some of her other personal experiences with me, as well as those of her father. He used to live in an old colonial home in Middletown, and discovered that not only his house, but the area itself, are indeed quite haunted...

• • •

Amelia: At what time after moving in did the paranormal events start happening with your father?

Kim: The moment he moved in, strange occurrences began. Shortly after moving in, after some unpacking, he went to bed and later awoke to loud sounds coming from the kitchen. When he went to investigate, he found that bottles of wine that had previously been on top of the refrigerator were lined up on the floor on the opposite side of the room.

A few months after that, my father began waking up in the morning to find the house being very cold. He would check the thermostat and found that it had been turned down to below 60 degrees during the night. After a few mornings of this happening, he decided to put duct tape down to hold it still, thinking that maybe vibrations were causing the thermostat dial to move. The next morning he woke up and the room was so cold he could see his breath.

He checked the thermostat and found that the thermostat had been turned down but the tape had not been moved.

Amelia: Did you ever experience anything in the house?

Kim: One day I went to visit him and spent the night. Sometime early in the morning, I woke up to the sound of black powder rifles going off. My dad started looking into the history of the area and found out that the Battle of South Mountain had occurred near there. This is in the same region where many interesting legends originate.

Amelia: Did your father ever have an experience with any of the "legendary" spirits of the area?

Kim: Well, one day, when he was out mowing the grass, he saw a woman in a blue dress standing near the driveway. He stopped mowing and began walking toward her, thinking she had a question about a nearby property for sale. He got about ten feet away from her and she turned and walked into the side of a hill. I'm not sure if she was the White Lady, but I am sure my father did not believe in ghosts until that day.

Amelia: I can't blame him. Did he ever talk about any other paranormal experiences occurring in the house or the area?

Kim: Yes. There was a woman my father started dating who he had known since high school. One night she left late and was driving home. As she drove down the mountain, a child on a bicycle came out of nowhere and rode right in front of her vehicle. Thinking she had hit the boy, she stopped and got out, only to find no one around. She called out to the boy and heard nothing but the night.

The next morning she called my father to tell him what happened. He asked a few of his neighbors about it, and found out that years ago a boy had been riding his bicycle on the road and died when he was hit by a car.

I'm sure other things may have happened while my father lived up there, but those are the main incidences that I can vividly remember.

THE OLD YELLOW HOUSE
Riverdale, Prince George's County

Paranormal investigators come to the field in the strangest of ways. Sometimes their journey brings them from a point of healthy skepticism and a simple desire to learn more about the paranormal. Sometimes people begin with a passion for folklore that urges them to reach beyond legend and investigate other possible origins of spirit phenomena. And sometimes, a strong paranormal experience or history of experiences is all it takes. A classic example of this is someone moving into a haunted house.

Margaret Perry Ehrlich is the founder of Inspired Ghost Tracking (I.G.T), the ghost hunting team featured earlier in the story entitled, "The Dr. Samuel A. Mudd House." She was raised in Riverdale, a bustling suburb of Prince George's County near Washington, D.C., in a neighborhood of single family homes. In her own words, she tells of her experiences growing up in "the old yellow house…"

• • •

The old yellow house was located in old Riverdale and built in 1920. It's a house that will always be remembered. It was the late 1970s and I was only 12 when my family and I moved into the house. It was two stories tall with two living rooms, a kitchen, breakfast nook, and a pantry downstairs. Located upstairs was the master bedroom on one side of the hall, with four connecting bedrooms on the other.

My mother, five brothers, our friend Terry, and I all lived in the house together. It didn't take us long to realize there was something or someone living with us that didn't belong.

Strange things started to happen almost right away. One evening, after everyone in the house had gone to bed, Terry came home from a late date. As she walked towards her room, she noticed that the attic door in the ceiling was open. No ladder or chair was visible to explain how or why it was open. The next morning she awoke before the rest of us, and then found the attic door had been closed.

This was only the beginning of the attic door opening and closing on its own. There were times when my mother would find it open and ask one of the boys to close it, only to find it open again later.

Another mysterious event that happened in the house concerns my mother's bedroom door. The door had the habit of opening by itself, so she started locking it at night before turning in. Several times, even though it was locked, the door would then unlock again and open on its own. She tried everything she could think of to keep the door locked and closed, but to no avail. Another problem door was a balcony door located in my older brother's room that would also open on its own.

No surprise here, but I feel compelled to mention that the cellar door would also open and shut. It had been used to store coal back in the day. Being cold, damp, and dirty, it was in every way like any other creepy cellar in the world. If you own an old house, you know what I mean.

Night after night for several months, I would also lie awake feeling as if someone were watching me. The room next door was occupied by Terry, who had been a very healthy person before moving into the house. She was soon mysteriously plagued by various illnesses. We decided to switch rooms and within a few nights, Terry's illnesses began to fade and she started to have restful nights again.

I then started to become ill (but not because of the room, for different reasons) and had to stay home from school for several weeks. One evening while I was home alone, I was in the living room watching TV when all of a sudden the dog jumped up and started to bark at the stairs that led to the second floor. Being the only one home, and scared, I decided to investigate my dog's actions.

Halfway up the stairs was a landing with a full length mirror on the wall. Much to my surprise, I noticed the mirror reflecting the image of a woman in an old-fashioned gown.

Being just a child at the time, it is hard for me to remember all the features of the woman, but she was maybe in her thirties with long brown hair all put up on her head, and she was tall and skinny.

Petrified, I took the dog and sat on the front porch until my brothers came home. Relieved when they finally arrived, I told them what happened and one of my brothers then told me what he was experiencing in *his* room.

Being an old house with minor renovations, our ceilings had been replaced with drop ceiling tiles (like the sectioned panels found in classroom or office ceilings). At night, my brother would lie in bed and watch the ceiling tiles move…

He told me how the tiles would rise up, slide over, and then minutes later would slide back into place. He would watch them moving until he finally fell asleep.

Then one evening, my mother was in her room and heard something in the hall. When she went out to investigate, she saw a man and a woman all dressed up going down the stairs. Years later when we talked about the house, we decided it could have been the same woman that I had seen in the mirror.

Lastly, the dining room was home to one of our particularly eerie house guests. My family was taught to push our chairs in at the table after each meal. Several times when my mother had come downstairs, the chairs would be pushed away from the table as if people had been sitting in them. We could never explain how this happened and actually began to get used to our new "friends."

They had, after all, never done anything to harm us. Our "friends" also inhabited one of the living rooms used for entertaining guests. No matter how hot it was in the summer, there was always a chill in the air in that room. My mother would even try to light a fire in the fireplace but would fail with every attempt.

These are the events that took place in our home for the years that we lived there. We didn't stay there long, but it wasn't because of the haunting. The ghosts actually seemed quite friendly and they didn't mean us any harm.

I think living in this house is really what started my curiosity in the paranormal.

MRS. QUWEE
Baltimore City

It is widely believed that the innocence and openness of children make them more susceptible to paranormal encounters than adults. Often, children will have detailed and intimate interactions with ghosts, as if they are real living people. But many children who are able to communicate with ghosts lose this ability over time. Sometimes they barely recall or have no memory of their interactions.

Samantha Kelley is an up-and-coming ghost hunter and founder of Kelleyano Researchers and Investigators of the Paranormal (K.R.I.P.), the ghost hunting team featured earlier in the "Jericho Covered Bridge" story. She only learned later in life from her parents about her childhood experiences with a protective "imaginary friend" she had called "Mrs. Quwee." Like Margaret Perry Ehrlich and her experiences in "The Old Yellow House," Samantha is fascinated by her parents' stories and considers this period of her life, although she doesn't recall any of it, the pivotal starting point of her lifelong journey with the paranormal...

• • •

I have believed in the paranormal since I was a little girl. I believe that there are many different types of ghosts and spirits out there, from energy left behind, to intelligent spirits, to demonic entities. I started believing in the paranormal after hearing stories from my parents about my childhood and my encounters with a ghost at a young age.

The activity really didn't start happening until I was born. When I was little—from when I was born until I was seven (1990 to 1997)—we lived in an old house in Baltimore City, on Old York Road near Memorial Stadium. When we lived there, I had an imaginary friend named "Mrs. Quwee," as I would pronounce it—or at least my parents thought she was just imaginary.

Our house was a three-story white Victorian house built in 1906 with a three-quarter porch. It had no indoor plumbing when it was built. The house was one of two identical houses. The other house had burned down. Back in the day there was a farm restaurant and horses on the property. We found horseshoes buried in the back yard.

The activity started off normally enough. They would hear me talking to her or playing with her. Then they started to notice that my room would be the coldest in the summer and the warmest in the winter. One time they commented on how warm it was, and I said it was just Mrs. Quwee taking care of me! They thought that was weird.

Apparently every night the toilet seat would slam, over and over. Again, I told them it was Mrs. Quwee. My dad even duct taped it shut one night and then woke up to hear it slamming, with all the duct tape ripped apart.

Sometimes, pictures would fall and the glass would break, but all of the glass would be in a pile on top of the broken picture. I would say it was just Mrs. Quwee protecting me.

After we moved, I never spoke of Mrs. Quwee again. After hearing these stories, I became interested in the paranormal and started reading about it and watching shows about it. My fascination with the paranormal spilled over to my little sister, you know, since she wanted to be just like me. We would always watch all of the shows, drawing our own conclusions as to what was real and what was TV magic.

We now live in a home with a double lot and a huge back yard, with a parking lot at the end of the yard that separates our yard from a church and graveyard. One night this summer [2011], since I'm back from college, my sister, her best friend, and I decided to go to the graveyard with our video camera and a digital recorder. Just to see if we could find anything, for fun.

After catching some weird voices, we played them for my dad—who is the biggest skeptic—and he was kind of shocked. Well, the three of us were bitten by the paranormal investigation bug and decided to make an investigation team.

Being told about Mrs. Quwee started my fascination with ghosts and finding out what's on the other side. If it weren't for my experiences with her, I may never have become interested in ghosts.

A HOUSE ON SATYR HILL ROAD
Parkville, Baltimore County

Baltimore County is home to "Horse Country" and beautiful rolling hills, streams, and forests. Centuries of rich history intertwine from well before the American Revolution up to present day. The homes, buildings, and architecture found around Baltimore County reflect the evolution of Maryland from a colony to a modern state. Many of the places left behind by time are preserved by parks and historical societies, or kept hidden for thrill seekers to discover, and some are just regular residential homes.

Paranormal investigator Dina loves to explore her county, always curious about whether these old houses and abandoned places are still occupied by their former residents. She even has the awkward but inspirational privilege of living in a haunted house herself, located off of Satyr Hill Road in Parkville…

•   •   •

Me: What kind of house do you live in and are you familiar with its history?

Dina: It's a single family home that sits off of the road back near the woods. I have lived here for about 12 years. I'm not really sure about the age of the house, but I think it was built recently, maybe the 1950s. There is a story I heard that a man died here years ago, one of the first owners. I did not find this out until after all the paranormal activity started happening.

Me: Please share some of your experiences.

Dina: I have quite a few. When I first moved here, something just didn't seem right. It was just me and my kids, and I always got the feeling that I was being watched and that there was a "man" somewhere in the house.

I never saw him, it was just a feeling. We would also hear a lot of noises and things throughout the house and got a really bad vibe. Then one night I was home alone and I could hear someone walking upstairs. It was loud and definite. These footsteps threw me for a loop because when you step from one room to another, it makes a very distinct sound. This time, and then often after that, I would hear three and four footsteps, one after another. I would be terrified.

Another time, my mother was spending the night with me, and I was in my room downstairs, but could hear her talking to someone upstairs. So I went to see what she was doing. When I found her, she was at the top of the steps talking. I asked her, "Who are you talking to?"

She said, "I was talking to you."

I said, "I was in my room downstairs."

She told me, "No, you were just standing at the bottom of the steps, right here." But I hadn't been. She said that all she had seen was a black outline of person, but she really did think it was me.

So who she saw, I have no idea.

I also had a night where I was alone and I was sleeping on the couch. It suddenly felt like the whole room got really dark and I felt like someone was behind me. I was sleeping facing toward the back of the couch, and just felt like someone was standing right there.

I think this was the scariest incident for me because I could just *feel* that something was there. I have never been afraid of the dark or anything. I ghost hunt, but it was a strong feeling that I had never felt before. And it felt *bad*.

Finally I asked a pastor to come bless the house and the land. Since then, I actually haven't had any problems.

Me: What do you make of all these experiences?

Dina: I have had paranormal experiences throughout my life, ever since I was a child. I'm not sure what they mean. That's why I got into paranormal investigating. It's almost like a mission: now I have to find the truth.

THE GERMAN HOUSE AT HOOD COLLEGE
Frederick, Frederick County

Many of the buildings on the 50-acre campus of Hood College, a former all-female school in the heart of Frederick, are rumored or well-known to be haunted. Brodbeck Hall, the oldest building on campus, was built in 1868 and was a popular beer hall and saloon into the late 1800s. Today, Brodbeck serves as the college's distinguished music hall. Ghostly giggling, voices, the heavy footfalls of dancing boots, and phantom piano music are all said to echo throughout the halls at night.

Memorial Hall is one of the campus dormitories and home to a legend about a female student whose throat was slashed in the elevator. She dragged herself to her dorm room and in her dying moments, scratched at the door for help. Her roommate inside was too scared to open the door or get help, and the student's body was found the next morning, lying by the door with bloody scratches across it. While this is a fairly common college campus urban legend, dating back to around the 1960s and 70s, it is a fact that the Memorial Hall main elevator goes up and down by itself, even with students in it who have already selected a floor. Whether this is a trick of faulty wiring or the result of a grisly death is open to debate.

There are still other, less talked about haunted spots on the college's small but storied campus. I was a student at Hood from 2003 to 2007 and for the most part lived in a dormitory that was slightly off campus called the German House. This was a language immersion dorm designed to encourage students studying German to speak the language with each other and the native German teaching assistant.

The house had once been a private home on Magnolia Avenue and was acquired by the college and converted to a dormitory several decades ago. It held a maximum capacity of five students. The basement had also been a furnished apartment for the language assistant up through the 1970s, but was currently available just for storage.

I began living there during the second semester of my freshman year, but it was in my sophomore year that my housemate Kim and I started having strong paranormal experiences. Later, as a senior, my housemate Sarah and I continued to experience activity.

When I asked Kim to send me her most vivid recollections of the house being haunted, this is what I received…

• • •

There was a time during my sophomore year that my friends Chris, Daniela, Jordan, and I were in the basement. We were looking around and I had walked over to the couch. I saw a figure walking up behind me and I assumed it was Chris. I turned around to say something to him and realized no one was there. Everyone was standing over in the room with the water heater.

I remember hearing giggling and voices a lot, too. I even started locking my bedroom door at night because I was nervous about going to sleep alone. I also remember finding weird bundles of twigs rolled up with feathers a few times. I specifically remember finding one at the foot of my bed and one at the bottom of the attic stairs.

•   •   •

Sarah sent me a very detailed description of her experiences, leaving out only one—almost unbelievable— incident that we later learned we had both shared. I'll explain later, but first, here is her account…

Prior to living in the German House, I didn't really think about ghosts. It wasn't that I didn't believe in them, I just hadn't really considered their existence. Some people love to tell or read ghost stories because it's entertaining. But I never found it that exciting. I tend to be a more, "rationalize everything, be logical" type of thinker.

I moved into the house in 2006. The house was built in the 1940s, I'd say, based on what I know about the neighborhood. Also, the ceiling of the porch was painted light blue, and this was a popular trend of that time.

There were creaking noises from the first day I moved in. At first I just figured it was an old house with warped floorboards. It didn't seem unusual to hear noises from time to time.

However, after I had lived there for about a semester, there was one day when I knew I was alone in the house. I was absolutely sure my housemates were all in class, or work, and not at home. That day I was downstairs in the living room, writing a paper, when I heard someone walking around upstairs. It was a series of creaks of the floorboards that went on for at least a minute. The same sound as when a housemate would be home and upstairs walking around in her bedroom.

At first, being the logical thinker that I am, I figured a housemate must have cut class and come home through the back door. It was a good time for a break from my paper, so I went upstairs to say hi to her. But when I got to her room it was dark and locked, and she was not home.

No one was home in fact, just as I had previously thought. In retrospect, the back door was the loudest door in the house and always used to slam shut. If anyone had come home and entered through there, I would have heard it.

The incident was not frightening to me, just kind of perplexing. I was more curious as to what could have caused those footsteps. But my paper was not going to write itself, so back down to the living room I went.

I also heard more footsteps that day. And many more times after that, when I was alone in the house. There would be the sound of someone clearly walking around upstairs when there was no one doing any such thing. It became part of my reality.

The basement of the house was generally creepy, too. There would be this overwhelming feeling of unwelcome down there. It used to be a full apartment, with kitchen and everything years ago but was now empty and none of its rooms were used. There was space to store boxes if we needed to, but no one ever did. None of us liked going down there. It was as if we could sense something terrible, but didn't know what.

The German House at Hood College, a language-immersion dormitory that was once a private home. *Photo courtesy of Daniela Daus*.

The funny thing is we were all adults, upper classmen in college, so we were too old to be scared of old basements and footsteps, just on principle.

Toward the end of my junior year, I had one experience that confirmed to me there was something paranormal happening in the house. At this point I had just a general feeling that there was a presence that could not be explained. Again, it wasn't frightening, but felt more curious. I hadn't talked to any of my housemates about it because I had nothing that specific to be worried about. Then I actually *saw* something.

I was leaving my bedroom on the second floor, probably going to a lecture or work, and going downstairs and outside. Just as I got to the staircase, and my foot touched the first step to go down, I saw this object out of the corner of my left eye.

It was a black orb that just flew down the stairs in a split second. It started in my left peripheral vision and then was suddenly in front of me, at the bottom of the stairs with me at the top.

Just as the orb reached the fire door at the bottom of the stairs, it made a noise, as if it were solid and had just "smacked" into, or through, the door. This was not a door that could be left ajar, it was designed to be a heavy regulation metal fire door.

The "orb" itself was ethereal looking. It was a little smaller than a volleyball, but not solid looking. The best way to picture it is when you unplug the cable on your TV and you just get that black and white static. It looked like a sphere of that static.

The whole thing took a spilt second. And while, again, I was not frightened, this was not easy to get out of my head. I went to the lecture, or wherever it was I was going. But I couldn't shake it as easily as I could the repeated footsteps, mostly because I had never experienced anything like it. I'd never seen something that I couldn't explain. And if it were my eyes playing tricks on me, what about the noise at the exact moment the orb met the door?

There was something or someone in the German House that couldn't be explained within the realm of normal. Whether it was a ghost or a spirit or whatever you want to call it, something was in that house. But since the presence was never really threatening, I went on living with it. By the time all this had happened, the college year was almost over, and I would be moving out soon for the summer anyway.

Since living in the house, I have never experienced anything like what I experienced there. But I do view life and death in a different way.

• • •

Now, this is what I experienced during the years I resided in the house. During my sophomore year, Kim and I lived with our language assistant and friend Daniela. The three of us had another housemate upstairs who mostly kept to herself. She was very friendly but had a reputation on campus for being strange. She had the attic room, which spanned the ceilings of all three of our bedrooms on the second floor. We would hear talking up there—in different voices—when we knew she was alone, and heard other loud sounds, like someone rolling something very heavy from one end of her room to the other. Sometimes noises would come from up there in two different places at the same time, again when we were sure she was alone. We were all convinced this girl had something to do with the sudden upstart in activity.

Kim's friend, Jordan, who later became my friend, would come to visit us and watch our television in the living room. He and I weren't particularly close at the time, but one night he came running up the stairs to my room. He was out of breath and asked if he could hang out with me for a bit because he had just seen an apparition in the hallway downstairs. I was shocked but trusted him because I knew him to be a reasonable person who would also not want to embarrass himself in front of a girl.

When I was alone in the house at the end of my sophomore year, I heard who I thought was our strange housemate come down the stairs and "scamper," with a distinct whooshing sound, through the living room toward the front door. I was in the kitchen at the time and even thought I saw, out of the corner of my eye, the heavy fire door that led from the staircase to the living room closing, as if someone had just come through.

When I realized there was no one there, and she was nowhere to be found, I was overwhelmed by such a feeling of fear that I left the house, sat in my car, and called my mom.

We would also often hear footsteps throughout the creaky house and I always had the feeling of being watched by someone in the downstairs area who was "waiting" for me to leave. We would hear the sound of feet moving across carpet coming into our rooms, and would turn around to greet each other only to find that no one was there. Even Daniela admitted to hearing these noises and feeling a presence.

I left to study in Germany for my junior year and returned to the German House as a senior. During this time, I lived in the house with Sarah and our housemates Chelsea, Michelle, and the language assistant Sven. Chelsea, Michelle, and Sven never reported anything out of the ordinary.

I was often tired and stressed out, not yet knowing that I was suffering from the late stages of Hodgkin lymphoma (for which I was later treated and fully recovered from). I would stay in the house alone at night while my roommates were out having fun. Once, while I was alone and in bed trying to fall asleep, something in the middle of the room caught my eye and I was suddenly aware that there was a solid black "orb" hovering about five feet away from me and five feet off the ground. It was like a small floating bowling ball. After watching it for a few seconds, it shot towards my door, which was a school-regulation steel fire door. When it made contact with the door, I heard a loud cracking sound that made me wince.

Sarah and I knew we shared a strange floating orb experience in the house, but the most astonishing thing that happened to each of us was not something we discovered until several years later during a casual conversation about our old college days. Rewinding back to my sophomore year, I had lived in the largest room on the second floor. One night, I had a bad night terror accompanied by sleep paralysis. Sleep paralysis is sometimes called "Old Hag Syndrome," and involves a brain-to-body interaction that somehow causes the body to become numb during sleep and feel paralyzed. It's often accompanied by hallucinations or visions that can be interpreted as, and are considered by some to actually be, paranormal experiences.

During my sleep paralysis experience, I woke up but was unable to move. I watched a woman with long black hair, in a dark flowing dress, come out of the bedroom closet directly to my right. At first she didn't see me, but when she did, she turned and began screaming at me. She didn't make any sound, however, but her face became distorted in anger. She kneeled at the foot of my bed, pointing at me and shouting until my paralysis broke and I could just move the tips of my fingers on my right hand. After briefly looking down at my hand, I looked back at where she had been and she was gone.

I was horrified by the experience that night and the morning after, but never though much more about it. That is, until Sarah told me that she also had a night terror and sleep paralysis experience in that room, two years after mine. She stayed in the room during her junior year (my senior year). One night, she was lying in bed awake but unable to move, and a woman with long black hair in a dark-colored dress came out of that same closet and crouched at the foot of her bed, screaming and snarling at her but making no sound.

To say that we were shocked and frightened when we realized this had happened to both of us would be a drastic understatement.

Sarah and I have remained close friends and I wonder if the activity in the house revolved so much around us because of that. My cousin Melissa attended Hood after I graduated and also lived in the German House. She told me she and her housemates never experienced anything out of the ordinary.

It sounds strange, but overall I believe that the spirits in the German House were really watching over us. I certainly can't say the feeling was a compassionate or friendly one, but it felt as though they had begrudgingly accepted responsibility for keeping an eye on a bunch of unruly college students, one of whom was very sick and didn't know it yet.

THE DEVIL IN HAGERSTOWN

Hagerstown, Washington County

Some people seem to naturally attract spirits, and experience paranormal phenomena throughout their lives, including in their own, otherwise non-haunted homes. They are what some refer to as "haunted people." With the spirit world being full of a range of beings that have positive, benign, or even negative intentions, haunted people never know who or what they will encounter next.

I believe that my Uncle Bernie is a haunted person. He sent me many stories for this book, including the following in a handwritten letter. This is one of very few stories I received that actually involves a hostile entity, one that brought with it a distinct feeling of evil that my uncle truly thought to be a demon or even "Death" itself...

• • •

I had been diagnosed with a major immune system breakdown in April 1988, and was so challenged that I was bed-ridden for almost seven months. I had 16 doctors working with me, and 12 of them advised to me to get my affairs in order, as this year might bring my last Thanksgiving and Christmas. I fired those 12 doctors.

Being exposed to "agent orange" in the western mountains of Vietnam for 73 days on a recon mission near the Ho Chi Minh trail all those years before had finally taken its toll on me.

I also became single in October 1988, and at the time of this incident I was living in a 100-year-old townhome apartment in north Hagerstown.

I had taken medical retirement, having been diagnosed with a number of serious illnesses that had contributed to that immune system breakdown, including fibromyalgia. I had and was experiencing an episode of extreme pain and fatigue that lasted over two weeks.

The time was approximately 3:15 a.m., which is a time that seems many nighttime paranormal experiences occur. The 3 a.m. hour is sometimes called the "devil's hour." I was in bed, trying to sleep, but I could not sleep.

I heard the chain on the inside of the back door begin to rattle, as if someone was entering my residence. I reached for my revolver.

I heard, and could almost feel, heavy footsteps advancing down my hallway, past my library, and toward my bedroom.

Before me appeared a large black, translucent form, approximately seven feet tall. My ceilings in that townhouse apartment were about nine feet tall for reference.

I sensed that the "form" before me was a masculine one, and it was not the first time I had ever sensed it, but it was the first time I had ever seen it. Was it "death" or "the devil" that I had before me?

My heavy pistol was, of course, of no use to me at this moment.

I greeted the "vision" with the verbal demand to leave me and leave my home, for dying was not an option. The black form seemed to change shape as I yelled at him. He wasn't going easily and neither was I, as I had survived so much already and still had so much to live for.

After approximately ten minutes, I saw my clock, it was 3:25 a.m., and my "visitor" slowly turned away from me. I could hear his heavy footsteps walking back down the hall. They were so strong, yet it seemed he had been hovering in the doorway with no feet to touch the floor.

He entered my kitchen, and I could hear the chain rattle again on the back door as he left.

The next thing I recall was the sun coming up. I still had my pistol in hand and I rose from my bed to reconstruct, at least in my mind, what had occurred only a few hours earlier.

I had nice wooden floors and sectional rugs. The rugs had been disturbed as if someone or something had ruffled them up, and a few of my books that had been on the glass coffee table had been knocked to the floor. Perhaps due to the vibrations caused by those heavy footsteps.

—B.W.M.

THE LOG CABIN
Ellicott City, Howard County

My dad moved into a log cabin on New Cut Road in Ellicott City in the late fall of 1980. He was only 22 and had never left the state, much less been outside of the areas in Baltimore City and Carroll County where he grew up. When his friend Tom offered for him to move out there, and work and take classes at the local community college, it was an intimidating, risky, and unprecedented move for him.

The cabin had been built sometime in the 1950s and sat atop a hill on 52 acres of forest. It was part of a property that had once been used as some kind of boys' club or summer camp. About 400 yards down the hill from the cabin was an abandoned swimming pool, filled in with leaves and debris, and an old swing set. There was another empty building nearby that had also been used in conjunction with the camp, and the log cabin had been the main meeting point or lodge for the entire campsite.

There were two regular residential houses further down the road, built in the early twentieth or late nineteenth century. They were big but fairly dilapidated and were rented out by some young guys as multi-story bachelor pads.

Also close by was Taylor Manor, a psychiatric hospital which is now a modernized part of the Sheppard Pratt Health System. According to my dad, Taylor Manor was *the* creepy place in town back then. They were apparently still giving electroshock therapy and other controversial treatments to patients. His roommate Tom had been an orderly at the hospital but quit after two weeks because, in my dad's words, it was "a horrible and depressing place to be."

My dad seems to recall that the property he lived on was also somehow connected to the numerous mental health care facilities in Ellicott City—that maybe the boys' camp was specifically a getaway for troubled youth or young men with disabilities, but he can't confirm that.

In any case, once he got settled in to living in the cabin, he really liked it. Ellicott City was a cool place to be at the time and he enjoyed it, but it wasn't easy to get used to the view. All he could see from his cabin during the day was the woods, and at night, blackness.

The cabin was large and had a screened-in front porch with a spacious central living room. There were two bedrooms on the one side of the living room and a kitchen and bathroom on the other side. There were no curtains on the windows, no carpeting, no amenities, and they had absolutely no money.

They had a 13-inch black and white television and a small cassette player. They kept the heat on 50 degrees in winter and sometimes in the middle of the night my dad would get up and have to throw up in the backyard because he hadn't eaten in two days.

The cabin had a long driveway that sat at a 45-degree angle and was frozen in the fall and winter, forcing my dad to park at the bottom and walk through the woods to get home. He says there was a 20-foot long bridge he had to drive over, and then he would park and cross some wooden planks going over a stream and navigate through the trees up to the cabin. If it was nighttime and there was no moonlight, he'd have to feel his way home. It would be so dark that he couldn't see the cabin.

For the first two months he lived there, he had trouble sleeping because it was so quiet, and so utterly dark.

His paranormal encounter occurred a few months into living there, in the late winter of 1981, around February or March. He was alone in the cabin and in his bedroom studying for one of his classes. He didn't have the television or any music on. Everything was silent, and suddenly something just didn't feel right.

He calmly got up and went into the living room to read, but something still wasn't right. "I just had this eerie feeling suddenly," he said. "I started to look around the cabin apprehensively. I made a right to go into the kitchen after checking Tom's room. There was a front door in the living room and another door in the kitchen we never used, with no curtains on the windows. Looking into the kitchen, and out into the dark, I *felt* it."

He could see into the bathroom from there as well, and with the bathroom door open he could see the toilet and the sink. The door was about three quarters of the way open.

"I remember standing there thinking suddenly that there was *someone* behind that door. I wasn't going to walk in to find out. I was scared. I mean *scared*. I dashed out to my car and left. I actually drove to a shopping center and sat there for a couple of hours until I thought it was safe to go back. I just sat in my car waiting."

When he got back to the cabin, his roommate Tom was home and everything felt okay again. After that, he never had another experience.

My mom says that when she used to go visit him there, she would park by the bridge and look over at the empty swing set. With the swings sometimes moving by themselves in the gentle breeze, she would have strong feelings of sadness and loneliness, and wonder about the boys who used to play there.

My dad moved out of the cabin in July 1982, when he married my mom. I asked him if the cabin is still there, and he told me he drove by once not long ago to check it out, but apparently the whole area is covered in brand new houses. The cabin and the campground for boys—and their mysteries—are now gone.

MRS. HARMON'S HOUSE
Westminster, Carroll County

My parents moved into their first home in Westminster when I was just a baby. Here, they had several encounters with a ghost they never saw, but who made her presence very well known to them. I was too young to remember any of it, and am thankful for it now, especially after hearing my mom's stories about the house and meeting Mrs. Harmon.

My parents moved into the late Victorian row home on Green Street in 1986, when I was about a year old. My grandmother (my mother's mother) moved in with us and helped care for me while my parents worked.

The house, already about 90 years old at the time, had formerly been owned by one Mrs. Harmon, whose name was still etched into the original brass knocker on the front door. According to a conversation my mom had with their landlord, Mr. Reed, Mrs. Harmon had been a nice elderly lady who had lived in the house her whole life and had passed away peacefully at the hospital not long before we moved in.

The house had three stories—an unfinished basement with a dirt floor and a first and second story with original hardwood floors. One interesting feature of the house was that, although it was small, it had several staircases. The main stairway connected the living room to the upstairs with a small landing halfway up. My parents' bedroom was next to the top of those stairs.

There was a servant's stairwell located next to my bedroom door, which led down to the kitchen. Each end of the stairwell had a door with a small window. My parents almost never used it because even with both doors open, the passage in between was always very dark.

There was still another staircase *in* my room. My parents chose my room for me because it had a sun porch with large windows that I could use as a playroom. The first floor, next to the kitchen, had an identical sunroom and there was a staircase connecting my porch to that porch below.

In the first year or so of living there, my mom says the only person who really experienced anything was my grandmother, who stayed in a bedroom with no windows in the center of the second floor. My grandmother became interested in the occult later in life and would claim to see "visions" of Mrs. Harmon. She would also feel someone standing over her and breathing on her as she slept at night—pitch black with the door closed and all the lights off.

She was never afraid though. My mom feels that because my grandmother was also aging and ill at the time, as well as open to the paranormal, that perhaps Mrs. Harmon might have felt a connection to her and had an urge to watch over her or be near her.

Sometime around 1988, when I was three years old, my mom received a phone call from Mr. Reed one evening, asking if she had "seen her yet." When my mom asked who he meant, he replied, "Mrs. Harmon, of course." My mom asked him if that was a joke, and why he hadn't said anything about a haunting when they first moved in.

He assured her it was no joke, but he was apparently an eccentric old man and didn't have much more to say about it than that.

My mom shared this with my dad, and needless to say, it bothered them both. She is convinced today that once they opened their minds to the *possibility* of the house being haunted, Mrs. Harmon was able to reveal herself to them.

My mom points out that around this time I also started telling her and my dad about how I didn't feel comfortable in my room. I was apparently bothered by how many doors and windows were in there. I would tell her I could hear someone moving around in my room at night and touching my stuffed animals. After Mr. Reed's phone call, she started to take my concerns more seriously.

My mom says that while she never believed Mrs. Harmon meant us any harm and was only keeping watch over all of us, she and my dad went on to have two frightening encounters with her that they will never forget. I'll let her tell the story, as she told me…

• • •

It was wintertime. Your grandmother was in the hospital having her monthly blood transfusion. Your dad and I were at home, not working, and had put you to bed and gone to bed early ourselves.

It was around 10 p.m. and we were starting to drift off to sleep. All of a sudden, Dad said, "Shhhh," just like that.

I asked him, "Jim, what is it?"

He said, "Shhhh."

We lay there perfectly still, and it was then that I heard that first footstep at the bottom of the creaky wooden staircase. We listened to each slow, deliberate step coming up each individual stair. Slowly, like how an old woman would walk.

We started shaking, we were so scared. The house was locked up tight. No one could have gotten in and we just knew instinctually at that point that it wasn't someone from the outside.

As "she" approached the landing on the first set of stairs, we literally started pulling the blankets up over ourselves. At that point we were frightened to death but still thought it might go away.

I asked Jim again, "What *is* it?"

"Shhhh," was all he said.

Then she began to ascend the second flight of stairs, slowly. Again, we could hear every footstep and the loud creaking of those stairs all the way up. Jim said, "God, Louise, I think it's her!"

The final step on the top floor was right next to our bedroom, right outside the door. Finally, Jim shouted, "GO AWAY!"

I never knew him to be scared of ghosts or supernatural things. She never came any further. You see, we were afraid that if she had kept coming, we would actually *see* her. And if that had happened, we were going to have to move.

The next incident occurred the following spring. It was warmer—a chilled warm, so I know it must have been springtime. My mother was away again in the hospital for an overnight stay. I was off from work and had put you to bed. It was dark out, so it must have been around 9 p.m. Jim was at work.

An hour after you were put to bed, I was in the living room on the sofa watching television and waiting for Jim to come home. The front door was open with the screen door closed to let the fresh air in.

I started to hear footsteps from the upstairs coming down the hall from your room. Remember, the whole way upstairs was not carpeted and creaked all the time. But I heard distinctive slow walking from outside your door all the way down the hall.

I thought maybe you had gotten up and wanted to come down. I called out, "Amelia, are you up?" I didn't hear anything. If it had been you, you would have answered.

The footsteps continued deliberately, louder and louder as they—she—approached the top of the landing. From the sofa I was right in full view of whatever it was. I started shaking again, and I got up and ran through the living room, the dining room, and the kitchen to where the back stairs were that led to your room. I opened the door to the sun porch and called up those stairs to you. You didn't answer.

I went back in the living room and I actually heard the footsteps *continuing* and starting to come down the stairs!

I headed out the front door and sat on the front porch swing where I could look in the window, through the old lace curtains, and watch the staircase. I wanted to be outside in case I needed to bolt it to the neighbors next door.

But there was no one and no more footsteps. Jim came home at around 11 and found me still on the porch. I told him and was still shaking. He went upstairs and checked on you, and you were fine. He even looked in your grandmother's bedroom. Nothing was moved, nothing was out of place.

It was her. I know it as I sit here. I was wide awake that night and I know it was her. Her footsteps even sounded like she had on those big shoes that really old women wore back then, those big cushiony clog-type shoes that would insulate their feet. I couldn't have been imagining things.

•   •   •

My parents moved us that summer, after our four-year lease was up, to an apartment in Baltimore County where they could be closer to work. That's where my grandmother eventually passed away. What I find most interesting is that both times my mom or parents encountered Mrs. Harmon, my grandmother wasn't home.

I drove past the house in Westminster several years ago on my way to a college function, just to see my "childhood home," while I was in the area. The house is still there and occupied, so I didn't approach it. It had looked so gigantic to me when I was a little girl, but now just looks like a regular old-fashioned townhouse on an old-fashioned street.

A House Along The Miles River

St. Michael's, Talbot County

The Eastern Shore is undoubtedly one of the most beautiful parts of the state. Attracting thousands of tourists every year to its beaches and the Chesapeake Bay, it offers all the beauty of ocean and waterway landscapes, as well as sprawling farmland, open skies, and more incredible Maryland history. The further east you go, the older everything seems to get—great for historians, antique lovers, seaside romantics, and of course, ghost story lovers.

My friend Tina, whose other paranormal experiences were featured in the "Pry House Field Hospital Museum" story, used to spend long, idyllic weekends visiting a friend who owned a very old house on the Miles River in the vicinity of St. Michael's and a smaller town called Uniontown. The central section of the house was built in the 1670s, when Maryland was still a colony and most land west of it was considered frontier territory.

Guests arriving at the stately old house would first go into a large hallway that was built later in the late nineteenth century. The living room would be directly ahead of them, and according to Tina, this was the section of the house built in the 1670s, which at the time had been the entire house. To their left, guests would see a ground-floor bedroom, and to the right, they would see the kitchen.

The original, heavy wooden doors leading into the living room at the end of the front hallway had once been the main front doors to the home. The doors are now attached to the wall and fixed permanently open.

The main guest room was directly above the living room. This is where Tina would stay when she visited.

"The first time I slept there I was awakened soon after midnight by a series of distinctive noises," Tina told me. "A heavy wooden door was being opened, then closed. And not quietly, either—very loud. Then, for some time thereafter, I could hear the footsteps of several people walking around in the living room."

Tina could tell from the sound and vibration of the door opening that the movement had to have come from one of those seventeenth century doors, just below her, even though it would now be impossible to move them. "There was no question about it! I was freaked out the first time I heard the noises."

Equally as frightening were the footsteps. "I was sure that people were there who had a right to be there. The footsteps were 'normal' sounding and perfectly loud—not at all ambiguous! I was so startled that I rushed to a window at the front of the house to see whose car was parked out there! There was nobody, of course."

Tina discussed the incident with her friend the next morning and he explained to her with a smile that it happened all the time. "His explanation? 'Oh, a lot of the old houses here on the Eastern Shore are haunted.'"

Simply put.

The same thing happened to Tina almost every weekend she visited him after that. "I would hear one of the wooden doors downstairs open and then shut, and at least one person walking around downstairs for maybe half an hour. I never thought, 'What's that faint sound I think I hear, it sounds almost like footsteps.' No, it was clear. Once I got used to it, there were a few times when I crept downstairs to see if I could actually see a ghost there. Nothing, of course, and the wooden doors were always standing open—as they had been for probably a century. There was simply nobody there."

Part 3

BEYOND GHOSTS:

OTHER ENCOUNTERS
OF THE
PARANORMAL
VARIETY

DOPPELGANGERS
Wheaton, Montgomery County

The German word "Doppelgänger" refers to someone who is the "look-alike" of another person (literally: "double walker"). Paranormally speaking, a doppelgänger encounter involves seeing or interacting with an entity that appears to us as someone we know—sometimes ourselves. Doppelgängers are rarely seen while their living/human counterparts are also present, causing an encounter with one to range from being mildly confusing and seemingly without purpose to completely terrifying. This is an especially interesting paranormal phenomenon because it doesn't fit neatly into the "ghost" category.

I have heard quite a few interesting stories about doppelgängers. An acquaintance of mine in Chicago told me that she and her mother were sitting in her kitchen one day, when her husband came and sat down with them, and conversed normally with them for several minutes. Suddenly, she and her mother turned around and saw her husband come through the doorway into the kitchen. They both turned back around and looked at the table where he had just been sitting—and found that his chair was empty. Her mother speculated that the strange encounter may have been with her own deceased husband, who wanted to come to her and her daughter in a non-frightening way by taking on the form of her daughter's husband. Perhaps, and how very Freudian.

My Uncle Bernie sent me two letters detailing his doppelgänger experiences, one as an adult and one as a child. As an adult, he remembers sitting upstairs in their Altoona, Pennsylvania home one day waiting for his wife, my Aunt Debra, to bring up some tea and snacks. He clearly recalls seeing her come up the stairs with the tray of goodies and turn and walk into another room. He was about to get up and look for her when about twenty seconds later, the real Debra came up the stairs with the same tray…and asked him why he had such a puzzled look on his face.

Neither of the above incidences happened in Maryland but the one below did. This is Uncle Bernie's childhood doppelgänger encounter, which happened when he was six years old. It was around the summer of 1953. Uncle Bernie and my Aunt Patty were the only kids in the family so far, living in their childhood home on Valleywood Drive in Wheaton…

• • •

My sister Patty, three years old at the time, and I were playing "hide and seek" inside the house. Mom had brought us in from outside because it was extremely hot, and our house was nice and cool—and this was before air conditioning.

Patty was supposed to count to ten in her bedroom, if she could, and then try to find me. I hid in the kitchen, behind a tall trash can at the end of the kitchen counter. I had a good view into the dining room and living room.

Suddenly I saw what appeared to be my sister Patty come from the living room into the dining room and hide under the dining room table and chairs.

I left my hiding place and as quietly as I could, crept to the dining room entrance from the kitchen to try and scare her.

She was not there. I could still hear her counting out loud in her bedroom. I couldn't believe it!

Mom was in the basement ironing clothes at the time. I told her I was afraid of what I had just seen. Mom passed it off as me being out in the sun for too long.

That incident was imprinted on me, and I actually had feelings of a presence in our home until the day we moved.

—B.W.M.

UFOs In The Skies
Wheaton, Montgomery County
Frederick, Frederick County

UFOs are a fascinating phenomenon that causes us to wonder what's out there. They inspire awe, fear, paranoia, and plenty of conspiracy theories—either over possible alien invasions and abductions, or what our governments are up to and just aren't telling us.

Regardless of how we characterize them, UFOs have been spotted in the skies all over the world and continue to be reported every day. Maryland is a small state, but with its close proximity to the nation's capital, it is no wonder our state sees plenty of traffic from these mysterious spacecraft.

The advent of digital modification of photos and videos has all but destroyed the opportunity to present real evidence of the existence of UFOs, save for the government outright admitting that they exist...and making a whole lot of witnesses feel better and not crazy.

My Uncle Bernie's numerous encounters with the paranormal include three very detailed UFO sightings. Interestingly, the first two sightings occurred in the 1950s, when the U.S. was experiencing the height of its fascination with (and fears about) outer space. The Cold War, the space program, and a number of films speculating on the possible outcomes of alien invasions, including *The Day the Earth Stood Still* and *War of the Worlds*, captivated Americans.

His third sighting, which occurred more recently in 1993, took place over the vicinity of the Fort Detrick military base, near Frederick. This incident conjures up the common UFO question: are UFOs attracted to our armed forces and communicating with them, or are they actually designed by our armed forces, performing top secret missions that civilians must never find out about? I'll let you read the accounts below and decide…

• • •

It was the summer of 1958, and I was 11 years old, mowing our back yard at Vivian Place in Wheaton. My sister Patty came running for me, as something was wrong and my mom was very upset.

As I turned to head for the front yard, I saw Mom looking up at the sky.

At first I couldn't see anything, as I was looking too high. I reached Mom, and she said, "There Bernie, there it is, near the telephone pole by our driveway."

I looked and saw a large white "sphere" that had a bluish undertone to it. The sphere seemed to be drawing power from the electric cables in the telephone pole, as there was some sort of static line from the sphere to the cables, and a low crackling noise. It was amazing to see this in broad daylight.

I don't know how long the sphere had been there. Mom seemed unable to move, as if transfixed to the site. After moments, the sphere drifted skyward and headed north until it disappeared.

Mom and Patty had seen it, your mother Louise and Uncle Chris had seen it, I had seen it, and your Uncle Tony was not born yet.

We finally got Mom to go inside to cool off. We put her in her favorite chair, put her feet up, got her some iced tea, and she started chain smoking cigarettes to settle down. I believe she was in shock.

One other neighbor child may have seen it with us, Gretchen, who lived across the street and always played with Patty and Louise.

I do remember late that night when Dad returned home from work. Mom tried to explain what we had seen, and she was still emotional. Dad asked me what I saw and I told him. The other children were already in bed. I doubt any of us got much sleep that night.

Later that summer, in late July/early August, I was preparing to head for the woods to go fishing and catch frogs. I looked up at the sky and saw a cigar-shaped object traveling from east to west at a great distance and at a tremendous rate of speed.

I compared the speed to a small airplane that was flying low in the same direction, and a jet plane, also flying in the same direction and leaving a vapor trail in the sky. The UFO seemed to fly "between" the two airplanes noted, yet not close to them at all.

I was amazed at the speed this UFO had. I watched it until it disappeared into some clouds, and I never saw it come out from the other side.

At the time, there was a lot of news about Area 51 in Roswell, New Mexico, that had people talking all about UFOs and possible invasions from Mars, etc.

I just thought it was neat and caught nine frogs that day.

Sometime in 1993, I was driving home to Hagerstown from Rockville. I was passing through Frederick on Route 270 and when I got about to where there was an overlook, I could see a circular-shaped object in the clear sky, standing still in mid-air, over Fort Detrick near Frederick. At first, since I was moving, I thought the UFO was moving, too. Not until I pulled my vehicle over and parked did I realize the UFO was not moving at all.

I stayed in my vehicle, and looked at the UFO through some hunting binoculars that I kept in the backseat. It appeared to be oval in shape, and grayish-brown in color. I observed it for about fifteen minutes until it seemed to disappear behind or into a cloud.

—B.W.M.

A FLYING SAUCER ON LOTTSFORD VISTA ROAD
Mitchellville, Prince George's County

When it comes to my family, we either have an attraction to the paranormal that runs in our blood, or the paranormal is hopelessly attracted to us. My Aunt Patty also had a vivid close encounter with a UFO as a teenager in the late 1960s. She remembers her awe-inspiring experience with humor, and has no fear of what may be out there. She not only wants to believe—she does.

Her encounter occurred on Lottsford Vista Road, a dark, secluded country road with its own infamous reputation among folklorists, ghost hunters, and young thrill seekers. Stories extend back to the 1950s of a Crybaby Bridge along the road, complete with sightings of a phantom baby and mother, as well as a haunted mansion, and hellish, almost supernatural twists and turns that dare nervous passengers to simply "survive" the road.

There are also numerous stories of run-ins with the legendary Goatman, a humanlike creature with the head of a goat (or the head and body of a goat, or simply a strange Bigfoot-like creature) that stalks the back roads around Prince George's County, attacking people, livestock, and pets with an axe. The legend of the Goatman is often tied into our cultural misgivings about scientific advancements; the Goatman was allegedly borne either from botched animal testing on goats, or human experimentation that occurred in the nearby and equally legendary Glendale State Asylum.

Setting aside myth and legend, my Aunt Patty witnessed what can almost certainly be considered the *mother*ship of all paranormal phenomena to be experienced on this secluded road—or any road, for that matter...

• • •

This memory is very vivid, as if it happened yesterday. I will never forget this magical, monumental moment. Since this happened, I have always believed we live among other life forms, and that there are planets inhabited by life forms superior to our own.

I am sure if our wonderful government would see this, they would come get me and put me in a home somewhere on a deserted island! That sounds pretty good to me actually, as long as they would provide the following: a shower, toilet, Chardonnay, a couple of horses, a garden boy to take care of the above...anyway...

It was a balmy summer night in 1966 and I was with my regular group of teenagers (add my brother, your Uncle Tony, age five—he was my little cherub and I took him a lot of places with me back in the day). I was 16, my best girlfriend Susan was 18, her sister Linda was 15, my boyfriend of the summer, Bob, was 16, and Barbie, our teeny, tiny little asthmatic friend who was the size of a mouse, (her inhaler was bigger than her) was 14. We were in a red and white station wagon.

This took place near Ardmore, Maryland on a road we all called, "The Branches." Its real name was Lottsford Vista Road. This was a country road, not a lot of houses, and the ones that were there were either set back in the woods or were little tiny homes that would make one wonder, "Does someone really live there?"

It was also a dangerous road, lots of curves, densely wooded, and inhabited with motorcycle gangs like the "Hell's Angels" and "The Pagans"—all of whom had made us their friends and promised to protect and take care of us if ever in danger. Boy, those were the days!

This was just the place nerdy teenagers like us found intriguing, mysterious, and fun to drive along. We would drive down to the deepest part of the wooded road area and turn off the car lights as we drove. It would be *so* dark, we felt invisible.

Anyway, on this night, we did just that, and on our way back home from scaring the poop out of ourselves, we were turning left onto Lottsford Vista Road and to our right was this huge red barn. We were all used to it because we were all very familiar with this road, of course. But on this night as we turned to go left, we all looked up and saw the most amazing gigantic, beautiful, silver dome with red lights dotted around the base, with white lights between the red ones.

It was hovering over the barn and was as big as big can be. The car actually *stalled*. Susan could not get it to start again. We were sitting there, staring at this "flying saucer" hovering over the barn, and Barbie, our mouse friend, suddenly whipped ten pencils out of her purse and started screaming in her asthmatic breath, "I'll save us!"

She started jabbing the pencils in the air, and Bob almost got stabbed in the eye, so we screamed for her to put her weapons away. We just sat there and continued to stare at the UFO as Susan desperately tried to start the car.

It was scary but at the same time I never felt threatened. I didn't scream, I just stared in wonderment and realized I had just witnessed a phenomenon. A surge of "Wow!" passed through my veins that night and I will never forget it. I feel privileged to have witnessed such an amazing sight.

The car finally started and we took off. The UFO was still there. We practically flew home ourselves. Susan's parents, who were government workers, were having a party that night and we all ran in the house and the first words out of Tony's mouth were (because he was just five), "We just saw a flying saucer on the dark road."

Well, Susan was grounded, not because of the UFO story, as the adults simply looked at us like we were crazy, but because she was not allowed to be driving back on Lottsford Vista Road. If the adults *only* would have known what they had missed that night! And even though Susan was grounded, that never kept us from going back to our spot to see if our visitors had returned. We were never that lucky again, but we always felt like other eyes were watching us as we drove through the darkness of the night.

GNOMES?

Hagerstown, Washington County

The word "gnome" conjures up warm (and sometimes creepy) images of the cheerful porcelain figurines that don red hats and kiss each other in the yards of grandparents everywhere. For those attuned to Paganism and other nature-based religions, as well as western mythologies, gnomes are described as any variety of small, nonhuman spirits that correspond to the element of Earth, and are closely related to leprechauns, fairies and elves. Together with other kinds of air, fire, and water spirits, they are called elementals.

Each of these has its own popular prototype and fairy tale image in modern culture, but mythologically speaking—and in paranormal terms—the lines are more blurred. Gnomes haven't always been viewed as cute little people wearing cone-shaped hats. They are historically thought of as shy, underground-dwelling beings that act as protectors of their land and are powerful when provoked. Thus, the modern concept of placing gnome statues in our gardens finds its origin in the nature of these beings as guardians, watching over us and bringing good tidings to our homes and harvests. They do not like to be seen, which would explain why they are so rarely spotted.

Altogether, the possibility of the existence of gnomes sounds at once very new age-y and comical. Yet people have reported seeing them, both in their traditional cartoonish glory and simply as small, humanlike creatures. There is even a theory that gnome and elf sightings are actually falsely documented alien encounters and are more common than we think.

Ghosts are easy to categorize as the spirits of people who have died. But what about beings such as gnomes, that were never alive and never died, and "exist" in our modern framework of understanding only in fairy tales and as magical symbols?

My Uncle Bernie documented two sightings of what we might call gnomes. One occurred in Pennsylvania, and will be included here only as a special addition to the first one that occurred in Hagerstown. Shocked to find these among the pile of paranormal encounters he and the other contributors sent me, I felt I could make one exception. But I will let him tell the tales…

• • •

I was traveling west on Route 70, heading for Altoona, Pennsylvania to visit my wife Debra sometime in the fall of 1996.

There are railroad tracks all around Hagerstown, which earned it its nickname, "The Hub," from the old coal and lumber days of the late 1800s and early 1900s.

As I approached the part of Route 70 West where railroad tracks pass under the highway, I noticed something down in the knoll by the tracks.

I slowed down. There was no traffic behind me. There sitting on the knoll was a man of childlike proportions. His head and nose were large, his body small, sitting hunched over, resting his forearms and elbows on his knees.

He was dressed in childlike clothing, with long-toed slippers, tights, a long shirt with a waist belt or rope, and he had a dark blue hat that reminded me of Peter Pan's hat. I could not believe my own eyes, and wished I had a camera.

His eyes seemed large and brown, yet a bit sunken due to his high cheekbones. His hands seemed unusually long for his size, fingers folded, yet he had large knuckles. I noticed him noticing me, as he glanced to his left. Remember, my vehicle was moving very slowly at this point.

I tried not to make eye contact with him. I didn't want to disturb him, and of course didn't want to wreck my vehicle. But then it happened: our eyes made contact and he, the "gnome," was gone in a flash, completely vanished.

I could not resist, I had to stop and investigate. Upon my arrival at the knoll, I went to the exact spot he had been. I noticed patches of grass were matted down and a few acorn shells were lying about.

I shared my sighting with Debra when I arrived in Altoona, but as you can imagine, I don't think she believed me.

My next experience with such a being happened in 2006 near Sankertown outside of Altoona, Pennsylvania. I was hunting deer on the McNeil Farm on Cresson Mountain with a friend. The morning was very cold, and we had a light dusting of snow. We had seen some very nice bucks during pre-season scouting using this trail a lot.

Around 8 a.m., I could hear something moving down the trail, in the woods behind us. I was prepared to see a deer travel in range, but I was quite surprised. What appeared was a "gnome," similar in all traits to the gnome I described in the other story.

I never took my rifle off safe, I couldn't imagine shooting it. The little person got to within 15 yards of me, and he either saw me or smelled me, I don't know which.

In a flash, he ran faster than any human or any animal I have ever seen. He actually became a blur as he kept on the trail.

I looked over at my friend, who was staring at me.

"Did you hear that?" Mike asked in a low voice. "Did you see anything?"

"Yes," I replied. "Not only did I hear it, but I also saw it. And you are not going to believe me when I tell you what it was!"

Mike had heard the approaching noise and had seen my body language as I had prepared for what may have been a nice buck. He heard the sounds getting louder and faster, yet he never saw the "gnome."

—B.W.M.

THE COFFIN FACTORY

Jarretsville, Harford County

The following story recounts perhaps my all-time favorite personal experience as a young and reckless suburban explorer, and will most certainly be one of those stories my grandkids will have to listen to over and over.

There was an old abandoned building beside the road near the intersection of Routes 23 and 165 in Jarrettsville. It was long and white, standing tall and slightly crooked in its rundown state, across the street from the E.G. Kurtz and Son Funeral Home, which is still in operation. It looked like an old-fashioned warehouse, and had trees and vines growing along one side.

I drove past it for a couple of years, wondering what it was, before some friends and I decided to check it out one night. We had never heard any stories about it, and it was not on the radar of local lore. We had pretty much exhausted other Harford County possibilities, having been to many of the well-known haunted or abandoned sites over and over, so we decided to give this place a try.

This facility in Jarrettsville, across from the E.G. Kurtz and Son Funeral Home, was once used to construct and assemble coffins. *Photo courtesy of Jarid Kranz.*

There were seven of us together on a cool, clear night, in about 2003. As usual, we were all ghost hunters, history buffs, and fans of old buildings and interesting architecture. Jen and a couple of my old friends featured in other stories in this book were present.

We parked behind the building, away from the lit road where a few cars would pass by on the country road throughout the night. Armed with nothing but flashlights, we decided to go into the building the old-fashioned way—through the front door.

The main door was on the front left side of the building, facing the road, and it was locked. This struck us as odd, considering the state of the building and the large hole in the door's window. It told us this was for sure not a frequented spot, just as we had thought.

Neil, a veteran of abandoned house exploration and a remodeler of old homes, reached his hand through the hole in the glass and turned the lock.

We opened the door and found ourselves inside of a large workshop, with a mix of modern and old-fashioned tools and trash strewn all over the desks and the floor. There was a very old adding machine on the desk immediately to our left, and a wall calendar from 1995 hanging on the wall behind it.

Directly across from us was a stairwell that had caved in, and on the right, a doorway leading into the next large room.

As we all stepped inside and got our bearings, Tif scanned her flashlight over everything around us. The floor, tables, and objects were covered in layers of thick white dust. It looked like the place hadn't been touched in years. We had stumbled upon a real gem!

Then she turned her flashlight up and shined it over the walls. We suddenly stopped and looked up in shock. On the far right wall were rows and rows of shelves containing small, child-sized coffins. They were unfinished and crafted of light-colored wood that had already been sanded and polished, and glistened in the beam of her flashlight.

Of course, it made sense. With a funeral home across the street, there needed to be a "facility" such as this to do the manufacturing. I had just never thought about or been able to picture what such a place would look like, or where it would be, and couldn't believe anyone would abandon this building and just leave all this behind.

Amazed, we began to explore the next room. It was another large room with high ceilings, and appeared to be the main work room. There were a great deal more unfinished child-sized coffins, and then several larger coffins in various stages of preparation. It was as if the work being done there had just stopped in time. At the end of that room was another staircase with lots of debris piled up in front of it and on it, and a small room to the left.

At some point I heard what sounded like a footstep or two coming from the upstairs. I ignored it because this was all too surreal as it was.

We were drawn to the room on the left and discovered that it had a single finished coffin inside of it, perched atop a stand. It appeared to be very old and the outside was covered in what looked like black or dark blue leather that was dry and peeling at the edges. No one dared to go in that room because the image of it was like something out of a horror movie or a fake haunted house, almost like someone playing a bad joke. There was clutter everywhere in the building except in this room. One of my brave friends and I were dared to go in and lift the lid off the coffin.

I went in, turned on my flashlight, and scanned over the top of it. It was barely as long as I was tall. I had noticed that with all the layers of dust covering everything, we hadn't seen any footprints on the floor or fingerprints on any objects. But when I stood looking down at the coffin with my friend on the other side of it, I saw a single set of three fingerprints on the top edge of the lid, just where I would have reached down to open it.

We both stood for a long moment looking down at it, and I decided I didn't want to open it after all. We may have been into abandoned house hopping, but I was a firm believer in not tampering with anything in them. We left that room and congregated in the main room, where I noticed even more tools and all sorts of wooden planks, coffin lids, and coffin shaped pieces of wood stacked against the walls.

Suddenly, Neil put up his hand and shushed us. He was the group skeptic and if he seemed worried, we listened.

"Guys," he said, "I think I've been hearing footsteps."

We were quiet for about one second and then the room erupted in whispers, all of us confirming that we had heard footsteps coming from the upstairs at one time or another, too. Neil even remarked about how the footsteps had seemed to "follow" us from one side of the building to the other.

But it was impossible for anyone to have been up there…the two staircases were blocked or nonexistent and it was obvious no one had been on the lower level for some time.

We all quieted down and held our breath. After just a few short moments and as if on cue, another distinct creaking came from right above us, like someone taking one long step.

"You guys," Neil said, "I think there is really someone up there. Like, a real living person."

With that, we scrambled to the front door and collected ourselves briefly. Neil was curious about something. Looking around, he shined his flashlight on the front door and spotted a light switch. "You know, the door was locked when we tried to get in. I'll bet you anything the lights work, too. I think someone is paying for electricity and that this place is still occupied."

He hit the switch and sure enough, the main overhead light came on. Mortified, embarrassed, and disoriented, we turned off the light, threw the door open, and ran around the back of the building to our cars. One of our friends had the courtesy and presence of mind to lock the door behind us as we fled.

As we got in our cars, Neil was explaining, half out of breath, that in his experience with abandoned buildings, he had learned that more people squat in them than we think. They will even work out a deal with the property owners to pay for the electricity or water, even if the place is in total disrepair.

Still confused as to how someone could access the upstairs to occupy it, not to mention be able to stay there alone with hundreds of coffins and coffin parts below, we saw a dilapidated and unto itself abandoned-looking car parked behind the house. Somehow we hadn't spotted it before, and there was also a ramshackle fire escape that made it possible—barely—for someone to walk up there and access an upstairs back door.

Our hearts raced as we left the parking lot, slowing down to look up at the front windows of the old building. There were no lights, no shadows, no signs of anyone there. We wondered if there really was a person upstairs, and if so, was he afraid of us? Did he wonder what we wanted, or was he just trying to mess with us?

I also wonder how just those three fingerprints appeared on the top of that coffin, with no other signs of human life anywhere else in the workshop.

This experience certainly taught me an important lesson about safety, as well as respect for private property and other people, both living and dead. Nevertheless, I treasure the opportunity to have such an amazing and unique story to tell.

This building actually still stands and has undergone extensive renovations. Please don't go there and try to get in. It's easy to spot and photograph from the road, and it's heartening to know that this place has been restored for use again.

I suppose it's always good to remember that when it comes to paranormal thrill seeking, sometimes there may be more than spirits watching you.

Part 4

GLIMPSES OF THE SUPERNATURAL:

BRIEF ACCOUNTS AND MEMORABLE MOMENTS

The following are very short stories or pieces of interviews and conversations, told in first person. Most of them are told anonymously, either at the storyteller's request or to lend them that bit of excitement (or skepticism) we feel when told the old story about that thing that happened to a friend of a friend...

A SERVICE ROAD IN BEL AIR
Bel Air, Harford County

"There was this place down a service road that's now a neighborhood, near the Festival Shopping Center, where, if you drove down it, you would find a lot of abandoned houses and a barn and lots of old cars. One night, my friend was out there late with one of his friends, driving on the service road to check the place out.

"It was raining and they stopped because my friend saw a frog in the road. He said to his friend, 'Oh hey look man, a frog!' And his friend pointed and said, 'Screw the frog— there's a dude standing right there!' My friend looked up and saw a weird-looking guy in jeans and a t-shirt just standing in the bushes. The guy then stepped toward the car and my friend panicked and floored it, backing his Jeep all the way out to the entrance of the road.

"He stopped so he and his friend could collect themselves. His friend said maybe the guy might need some help or something, so they decided to drive back to where he'd been. Sure enough, the guy was still there, standing in the bushes. Mind you, it was pitch black outside and raining.

"The guy stepped toward the Jeep again, they panicked, and backed all the way out again. It was a good quarter of a mile to drive in reverse. They collected themselves once again, figured they were overreacting, and decided to go back one more time. So they drove back, didn't see the guy at first, and then sure enough, he walked into their line of view. This time they panicked, did a three-point turn, and floored it to the entrance of the road.

"When they finally stopped the car and my friend hit the brakes, my friend looked into the rearview mirror and saw the guy standing *right* behind the car, illuminated by the brake lights. There was no physical way he could have moved that quickly, running a quarter of a mile in the rain down a bumpy, unpaved road at night with woods on both sides. They finally sped off—this time for good!" –J.K.

CUNNINGHAM FALLS STATE PARK
Catoctin, Frederick County

"Growing up in Frederick County, we often heard stories about military experiments and things that went on around Fort Detrick [in nearby Frederick] and Camp David [in Catoctin Mountain Park, next to Cunningham Falls State Park]. I have heard from several reliable people, including my own family members, that they have seen a Bigfoot-like creature in the park. People say it looks and walks more like a mutated chimpanzee, kind of lumbering on all fours and clearly a primate, but much larger. People think it actually has to do with military experimentation—something that got loose that shouldn't have." –C.L.

EAST MEDICAL HALL ROAD

Churchville, Harford County

The dead end of East Medical Hall Road is the site of a former tuberculosis treatment hospital that is now a patch of woods with some residential houses nearby. "We drove out there to see if the legend was true of ghost lights and shadow figures in the woods. The whole drive there was clear until we turned onto the road, and then it was incredibly foggy. The fog even seemed to take shape and the trees felt like they were closing in more and more the further the down the road we got. Once we pulled up to the dead end, it was pitch black in the woods ahead and we all swore we saw lights. We turned around and peeled out of there, feeling like we were being followed the whole way." –A.O.

A LODGE AT DEEP CREEK LAKE
Deep Creek Lake, Garrett County

"I was staying with several people in one of Deep Creek Lake's beautiful expansive vacation lodges. I slept on the couch in front of the large bay doors on the bottom floor. I was very comfortable and slept facing the doors with the drapes open.

"I was in a deep, restful sleep when I was suddenly awakened around 4:30 a.m. by a loud shuffling sound coming from behind the couch. It stopped and then after about five seconds, started again, a shuffling sound from one end of the room to the other. I lay motionless with my eyes closed, and decided it must be someone in our group who was confused and shuffling back and forth in an obnoxiously loud manner!

"I contemplated getting up to help them when the shuffling thankfully abated once again. I relaxed back to my sweet sleep and then it started again—shuffling from one end of the room to the other. I reluctantly opened my eyes, turned my head to peer over the back of the couch, and saw a white form go by. I determined that whoever it was finally found their bedroom.

"The next morning I had forgotten all about it. As we gathered at the breakfast table, my sister-in-law Kay asked me if I was in her room the night before. She had been sleeping in a room at the south end of the ground floor. Of course, I told her no. She stated that someone bumped against her bed, shuffled and hit her bureau, and then shuffled out of the room.

"As she said the word 'shuffled,' I suddenly remembered my experience. Kay and I interrogated everyone in the house and no one had been up roaming around at all that night."

–T.T.

PRIVATE HOME IN ELKRIDGE
Elkridge, Howard County

"A coworker of mine lives in Elkridge. He has three boys. He claims there is often weird activity that happens in his house, mainly electrical issues, cold spots, doors opening and closing, and so on. One day he was videotaping his children telling each other knock-knock jokes. One of the children kept asking, 'knock knock!' louder and louder. Later when he played back the video, he could distinctly hear a man's voice in the background asking, 'Who's there?'" –G.N.

JUDGE'S BENCH PUB
Ellicott City, Howard County

Judge's Bench Bar is located on Main Street in the heart of Ellicott City. "I had a friend who went there a lot and upstairs there is a pool table. He was playing pool by himself and said he had an encounter with something. After asking around he found out that the upstairs was 'haunted' by a woman who committed suicide. There are many theories on who it is. That area of Ellicott City has a bunch of stories. At one point about half the buildings went up in flames, killing some people. Many residents believe that the victims of that fire also haunt the area." –M.B.

HOUSE ON MOUNTAIN ROAD
Fallston, Harford County

"If you go down 152, past Route 1 near Fallston, kind of near this big restaurant with palm trees around it, there is a house that sits just below the road down a steep driveway so that you only see the top of the house as you drive by. One night at work, my co-workers and I were casually swapping ghost stories. When it got to be this one lady's turn, she became very serious and said that she and her family used to live in that house, and that something in the house was *evil*. She said the things that had happened there were so frightening and disturbing, she wouldn't even talk about them. She only said it was extremely haunted. Just seeing the look on her face and hearing the way she said it gave me chills." –J.C.

THE ADMIRAL FELL INN
Fell's Point, Baltimore City

The Admiral Fell Inn dates back to the 1770s and is located on the corner of South Broadway and Lancaster Street in historic Fells Point. "It used to a boarding house for sailors, and today it is an 80-room hotel. I'm an artist and was there taking some shots for my business, Tinshop Productions. My girlfriend and I experienced noises and really, really weird feelings.

"I especially couldn't be on the fifth floor for more than a few minutes. Every time I was up there, I kept feeling like I was about to pass out. My girlfriend had the same reaction. As soon as we got off the elevator on five, it totally felt wrong and the air was 'heavy.' We did hear that guests wanting a haunted experience should stay in Room 419, and hang out on the fifth floor.

"You could ask one of the ladies at the front desk—they might let you go up and check it out!" –Greg Baughman, Jr.

PRIVATE HOME IN HAGERSTOWN
Hagerstown, Washington County

This home is in St. James Village, near Antietam Battlefield. "I was in my downstairs family room reading when a solid white sphere appeared, coming out of the wall to the right of my fireplace. I observed the sphere move very slowly across the room, within five feet of me, and vanish into one of my bookcases. Instantly, I smelled my mother's perfume—Estee Lauder Youth Dew. The fragrance lasted several hours." –B.W.M.

CONCORD POINT LIGHTHOUSE
Havre de Grace, Harford County

The Concord Point Lighthouse and Keeper's Dwelling were built in 1827 and are located at the confluence of the Susquehanna River and Chesapeake Bay in historic Havre de Grace. Concord Point Lighthouse is the second oldest lighthouse in Maryland and one of the oldest lighthouses still in continuous operation on the East Coast. "I investigated the Concord Point Lighthouse in 2012 with my team, G-Force Paranormal. In March 1994, a young man by the name of Lance Alan Miles, age 34, was found dead outside of the Keeper's Dwelling, having suffered bullet wounds to the abdomen and head. He was found by the lighthouse caretaker, John O'Neill. According to the Havre De Grace Police Department, the body looked as if it had been dumped there, not killed there.

"The basement of the Keeper's Dwelling is where most of the paranormal activity has taken place, mainly noises, footsteps, and voices, and that's where most of our activity happened. We used the spirit box down there, which is a device that utilizes radio frequencies to generate spirit voices.

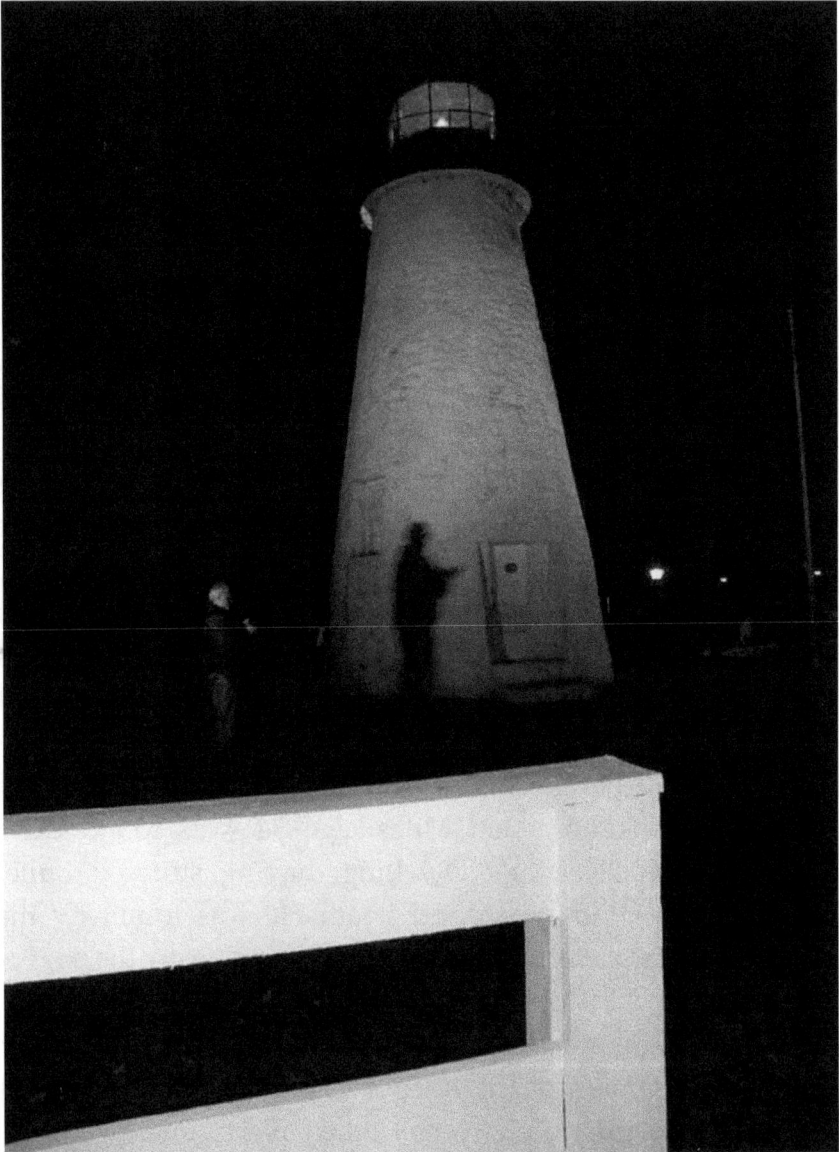

An investigator's shadow stretches ominously across the nighttime façade of the Concord Point Lighthouse in Havre de Grace. *Photo courtesy of Brenda Wilder Antlitz.*

The radio scans continuously on AM or FM and voices can come through. We had a very clear male voice come through the box, answering our questions as we asked them. We figured the voice was that of Lance Miles. Two particularly moving and eerie responses we got were when we asked how he was killed. He answered, 'Bad' and 'Help.' We left that night with many more questions than answers."

–Brenda Wilder Antlitz

PRIVATE HOME IN MT. AIRY

Mt. Airy, Frederick County

"My mom used to hear music and laughter in the basement. She would open the door and yell at the voices to quiet down, which they would do immediately! When my step-father moved in, there were many nights that the radios would turn on by themselves and wake us up.

"Throughout the years my family would talk about glimpses of people walking by, but my mother would see full apparitions. One night she woke up and found an old woman looking at her from her bedroom door. My mother told her to go away and the woman turned around and vanished. My mother woke up another time to find a man wearing a bowler hat staring at her through the window.

"Even now, footsteps can be heard walking up and down the stairs to the basement, and at times you can still hear the sound of our dog's tail wagging against the basement wall to be let up—our dog died in the basement in 1995 from a canine illness." –K.V.

PERRYMAN MANSION

Perryman, Harford County

Perryman Mansion is a secluded abandoned mansion on Perryman Peninsula, along the shores of the Bush River near a Baltimore Gas & Electric plant. "My friend was up there exploring at night. He told me that when he got to this one room on the second floor, at the end of the hall where everyone who goes there says they get a creepy feeling, he saw something come out of a dark corner. He said it was small, crouched low, and hissed loudly at him. He stumbled backwards and ran out of the house without looking back. He said he couldn't sleep that night and didn't have the nerve to go back to the house again until he had a big group of friends with him." –J.K.

STEVENSON AME CHURCH CEMETERY
Sparks Glencoe, Baltimore County

The Stevenson African Methodist Episcopal, or A.M.E., Church is located on Quaker Bottom Road. "We went out to explore the cemetery one night, and behind it, up the hill, are some woods. There were a bunch of us and we all felt really uneasy the whole time. The graveyard was creepy, as expected, and we even found a freshly dug grave, but all of us felt like we were being watched from those woods. The next day, we found out that a local man who had murdered his wife that night had fled on foot and was captured by the police—in those *exact* woods right behind the cemetery. All of us have always wondered if that strong feeling of being watched was actually him watching us." –S.P.

Part 5

RESOURCES AND REFERENCES

This section is meant to help you to do some more exploring and discovery on your own, whether simply to learn more about the paranormal offerings in your town or county, find others in your area with whom you can share your experiences, find help with a haunting, or even go ghost hunting.

I originally gathered an extensive list of places, websites, and paranormal groups for this section until I was overwhelmed by the sheer numbers in Maryland alone—and the possibility of omitting something and inadvertently offending someone. So I decided it was best to keep it short and sweet, and let you do the Googling.

Like the stories featured in this book, these recommendations merely scratch the surface of what's out there. But in case you feel like I still missed something, don't hesitate to send me an email. Tell me about your favorite haunted place, your website, your group, your sources, or your story!

RECOMMENDED READING

Big Book of Maryland Ghost Stories, Ed Okonowicz (2010): The title says everything. Okonowicz has written extensively on folklore in Maryland and the surrounding states, and can always be counted on for a good read.

Ghosts of Maryland, Mike Ricksecker (2010): Includes an awesome "Haunted Atlas of Maryland," which covers Maryland ghosts county by county.

Haunted Eastern Shore: Ghostly Tales from East of the Chesapeake, Mindie Burgoyne (2009): A great mix of ghostlore dedicated specifically to the legends and haunts of this historic region.

Monsters of Maryland: Mysterious Creatures in the Old Line State, Ed Okonowicz (2012): Features stories about Bigfoot, Chessie, the Snarly Yow, the Goatman, and more.

Spooky Maryland: Tales of Hauntings, Strange Happenings, and Other Local Lore, S.E. Schlosser (2007): This book will satisfy the folktale lover and covers many familiar legends, retold in their original contexts.

Weird Maryland, Matt Lake (2006): Part of the *Weird* series, this fun volume includes the full spectrum of legends, mysteries, ghost stories, creatures, UFOs, and interesting places in our state.

RECOMMENDED WEBSITES AND BLOGS

Maryland Mutual UFO Network
http://marylandmufon.com/
The one-stop shop for UFOs in Maryland. Learn all about UFO sightings in our state, report a sighting, or join MUFON and attend a meeting.

The Shadowlands
http://www.theshadowlands.net/places/maryland.htm
There are a lot of sites like this out there now, but this is one of the oldest and most thorough collections of personal experiences and local lore. You will have to sift through a lot of legends mistaken for facts, and just ignore the bad grammar. But the list of haunted locations is one of the best and most extensive there is.

Southern Spirit Guide

http://southernspiritguide.blogspot.com/

Great resource for stories and information. Get ideas for Maryland sites and beyond, and more good reading. Be sure to check the Maryland label, but consider snooping around in surrounding states, too.

Writing the Vision

www.writingthevision.com

An extension of her ghost stories, this blog chronicles Mindie Burgoyne's jaunts around the state and other places that are haunted or otherwise mysterious and interesting.

FEATURED HISTORIC AND PUBLIC PLACES

The Admiral Fell Inn
http://admiralfell.com/

Concord Point Lighthouse
http://concordpointlighthouse.org/

The Dr. Samuel A. Mudd House
http://www.drmudd.org/

Hell House
http://hellhouse.ellicottcity.net/

The Historic Elk Landing Foundation
http://www.elklanding.org/

Jerusalem Mill Village and Jericho Covered Bridge
http://www.jerusalemmill.org/

The National Museum of Civil War Medicine
http://www.civilwarmed.org/

Point Lookout State Park
http://dnr2.maryland.gov/publiclands/Pages/southern/pointl
ookout.aspx/

The Pry House Field Hospital Museum
http://www.civilwarmed.org/pry-house-field-hospital-
museum/
http://www.nps.gov/anti/planyourvisit/pryhouse.htm/

The Schifferstadt Architectural Museum
http://www.frederickcountylandmarksfoundation.org/fclf_s
chiffgen.html/

FEATURED GHOST HUNTING TEAMS

Cecil & Beyond Paranormal
https://www.facebook.com/cecilparanormalpage/

G-Force Paranormal
https://www.facebook.com/pages/G-Force-Paranormal/338304296283929

Inspired Ghost Tracking
http://inspiredghosttracking.webs.com/
http://www.meetup.com/inspiredghosttracking/

Kelleyano Researchers & Investigators of the Paranormal
http://www.facebook.com/Kelleyano.R.I.P/

PARANORMAL CONNECTIONS: MAKE IT PERSONAL

Ghost Tours

Baltimore Ghost Tours
http://www.baltimoreghosttours.com/

Ghost Tours of Annapolis and Baltimore
http://www.toursandcrawls.com/

Ghost Tours of Historic Frederick
http://www.marylandghosttours.com/

Howard County Ghost Tours
http://www.visithowardcounty.com/ghost-tours

Ghost Hunting Groups & Research Teams

The Online Paranormal Society Directory
http://paranormalsocieties.com/state_list.cfm?state=md

Note: The selected bibliography and resources used for the research of this book have been notated in this chapter under the "Recommended Reading," "Recommended Websites and Blogs," and "Featured Historic and Public Places" sections.

NOTE FROM THE AUTHOR

To my fellow paranormal explorers and adventurers: please remember to be safe, responsible, and ghost hunt in good company. Many of the places that have been discussed in this book are either private residences or businesses and establishments that have set hours…and strong opinions about ghost hunters! I encourage you to visit the places that are open to the public, but please do so lawfully and respectfully. And please consider leaving behind a donation where you can, so these places can continue to bring history and ghostlore to life for many years to come.

ABOUT THE AUTHOR

Amelia Cotter is an author and storyteller with a special interest in the supernatural, history, and folklore. Amelia lives and writes in Chicago but is originally from Maryland, where she earned a degree in German and History from Hood College. She has appeared on various radio and television programs, and regularly presents at conferences and events. Amelia shares her love for the *many* wonders of the world, while hopefully inspiring others to explore it, through her books, stories, poetry, and other writing. Visit her official website at www.ameliacotter.com, or write to her any time at ameliamcotter@gmail.com.

Other titles from Haunted Road Media in which Amelia Cotter has appeared:

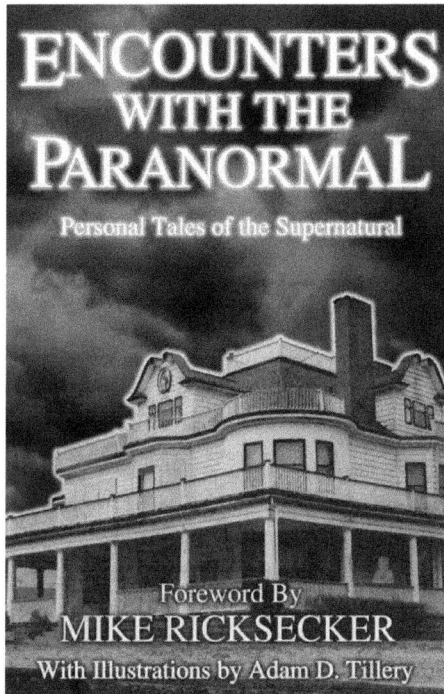

Almost everyone has a ghost story. Real people. Real stories.

Read about haunted houses and vehicles, experiences during paranormal investigations, visits from relatives that have passed on, pets reacting to the paranormal, psychic experiences, and conversations with full-bodied apparitions.

ENCOUNTERS WITH THE PARANORMAL reveals personal stories of the supernatural, exploring the realm beyond the veil through the eyes of a colorful cast of contributors.

For more information visit:
www.hauntedroadmedia.com